Langenscheidt

Patricia Highsmith
A Mighty Nice Man

Sechs Kurzgeschichten
von der bekannten
amerikanischen Autorin

Langenscheidt

Berlin · München · Wien · Zürich · New York

Wortschatzhilfen: Dorothea König

Internetadresse: www.langenscheidt.de

Druck: Druckhaus Langenscheidt, Berlin
Printed in Germany
ISBN-13: 978-3-468-44433-3
ISBN-10: 3-468-44433-8

1. 2. 3. 4. 5. * 09 08 07 06 05

Vorwort

Dieser Band mit Kurzgeschichten von Patricia Highsmith zeigt die Vielseitigkeit der amerikanischen Autorin. Sie zeigt sich in ihnen als eine genaue Beobachterin der Alltagswelt, mit einem ausgeprägten Gespür für die Abgründe der menschlichen Psyche.

Patricia Highsmith wurde am 19. 01. 1921 in Forth Worth/Texas geboren.

Ihren Durchbruch als Schriftstellerin hatte sie mit ihrem ersten Roman „Strangers on a Train“, der 1950 veröffentlicht wurde. Alfred Hitchcock erwarb für 6800 Dollar die Filmrechte daran („Zwei Fremde im Zug“).

Auf einer Europareise entstand die Idee zu Tom Ripley, einem Gauner und Psychopathen, der die Hauptfigur in fünf Romanen von Patricia Highsmith werden sollte.

Ripley mordet nur, wenn es unumgänglich ist. Er gibt sich gern als eine andere Person aus und kommt dadurch öfters in Schwierigkeiten, weil er die verschiedenen Persönlichkeiten nicht immer auseinander halten kann. Ripley wird durchaus sympathisch dargestellt.

Das Interesse der Autorin gilt auch in ihren Kurzgeschichten vor allem gespaltenen Identitäten und zwanghaften Verhaltensweisen. So handelt es sich bei ihr nicht um klassische Krimis, da sie besonderen Wert auf die psychologischen Konstellationen legt.

Wie bei den anderen Bändchen dieser Reihe werden die unbekannteren englischen Wörter mit ihren Übersetzungen und der Lautschrift in den Fußnoten aufgeführt, so dass die Texte für den Leser leichter verständlich sind und sich gut als spannende Freizeitlektüre eignen.

Langenscheidt

Inhaltsverzeichnis

Erklärung der Lautschrift

A Vokale und Diphthonge

[ɑː] reines langes a, wie in Vater, kam, Schwan: *far* [fɑː], *father* ['fɑːðə].

[ʌ] kommt im Deutschen nicht vor. Kurzes dunkles a, bei dem die Lippen nicht gerundet sind. Vorn und offen gebildet: *butter* ['bʌtə], *come* [kʌm], *colour* ['kʌlə], *blood* [blʌd], *flourish* ['flʌrɪʃ], *twopence* ['tʌpəns].

[æ] heller, ziemlich offener, nicht zu kurzer a-Laut, wie das kurze a in Quatsch, waschen: *fat* [fæt], *man* [mæn].

[eə] nicht zu offenes halb langes ä; im Englischen nur vor r, das als ein dem ä nachhallendes ə erscheint: *bare* [beə], *pair* [peə], *there* [ðeə].

[aɪ] Bestandteile: helles, zwischen ɑː und æ liegendes a und schwächeres offenes i. Die Zunge hebt sich halbwegs zur i-Stellung: *I* [aɪ], *lie* [laɪ], *dry* [draɪ].

[aʊ] Bestandteile: helles, zwischen ɑː und æ liegendes a und schwächeres offenes u: *house* [haʊs], *now* [naʊ].

[eɪ] halb offenes e, nach i auslautend, indem die Zunge sich halbwegs zur i-Stellung hebt: *date* [deɪt], *play* [pleɪ], *obey* [ə'beɪ].

[e] halb offenes kurzes e, etwas geschlossener als das e in Bett: *bed* [bed], *less* [les].

[ə] flüchtiger Gleitlaut, ähnlich dem deutschen, flüchtig gesprochenen e in Gelage: *about* [ə'baʊt], *butter* ['bʌtə], *connect* [kə'nekt].

[iː] langes i, wie in lieb, Bibel, aber etwas offener einsetzend als im Deutschen; wird in Südengland doppellautig gesprochen, indem sich die Zunge allmählich zur i-Stellung hebt: *scene* [siːn], *sea* [siː], *feet* [fiːt], *ceiling* ['siːlɪŋ].

[ɪ] kurzes offenes i wie in bin, mit: *big* [bɪg], *city* ['sɪtɪ].

[ɪə] halb offenes halb langes i mit nachhallendem ə: *here* [hɪə], *hear* [hɪə], *inferior* [ɪn'fɪərɪə].

[əʊ] mit [ə] beginnend und in schwaches u auslautend, keine Rundung der Lippen, kein Heben der Zunge: *note* [nəʊt], *boat* [bəʊt], *below* [bɪ'ləʊ].

[ɔː] offener langer, zwischen a und o schwebender Laut: *fall* [fɔːl], *nought* [nɔːt], *or* [ɔː], *before* [bɪ'fɔː].

[ɒ] offener kurzer, zwischen a und o schwebender Laut, offener als das o in Motte: *god* [gɒd], *not* [nɒt], *wash* [wɒʃ], *hobby* ['hɒbɪ].

[ɔɪ] Bestandteile: offenes o und schwächeres offenes i. Die Zunge hebt sich halbwegs zur i-Stellung: *voice* [vɔɪs], *boy* [bɔɪ], *annoy* [ə'nɔɪ].

[ɜː] im Deutschen fehlender Laut; offenes langes ö, etwa wie gedehnt gesprochenes ö in öffnen, Mörder; kein Vorstülpen oder Runden der Lippen; kein Heben der Zunge: *word* [wɜːd], *girl* [gɜːl], *learn* [lɜːn], *murmur* ['mɜːmə].

[uː] langes u wie in Buch, doch ohne Lippenrundung; vielfach diphthongisch als halb offenes langes u mit nachhallendem geschlossenem uː *fool* [fuːl], *shoe* [ʃuː], *you* [juː], *rule* [ruːl], *canoe* [kə'nuː].

[ʊə] halb offenes halb langes u mit nachhallendem ə: *poor* [pʊə], *sure* [ʃʊə], *allure* [ə'ljʊə].

[ʊ] flüchtiges u: *put* [pʊt], *look* [lʊk], *careful* ['keəfʊl].

Ganz vereinzelt werden auch die folgenden französischen Laute gebraucht: Die Nasale [ɑ̃] wie in frz. *blanc,* [ɔ̃] wie in frz. *bonbon* und [ɛ̃] wie in frz. *vin,* sowie die drei Vokale [o] wie in frz. *chaud,* [ɛ] wie in frz. *belle* und [ø] wie in frz. *monsieur.*

Die **Länge** eines Vokals wird durch [ː] bezeichnet, z.B. *ask* [ɑːsk], *astir* [ə'stɜː]. Die **Betonung** der englischen Wörter wird durch das Zeichen ['] vor der zu betonenden Silbe angegeben, z.B. *onion* ['ʌnjən].

B Konsonanten

[r] nur vor Vokalen gesprochen. Völlig verschieden vom deutschen Zungenspitzen- oder Zäpfchen-r. Die Zungenspitze bildet mit der oberen Zahnwulst eine Enge, durch die der Ausatmungsstrom mit Stimmton hindurchgetrieben wird, ohne den Laut zu rollen. Am Ende eines Wortes wird r nur bei Bindung mit dem Anlautvokal des folgenden Wortes gesprochen; *rose* [rəʊz], *pride* [praɪd], *there is* [ðeər'ɪz].

[ʒ] stimmhaftes sch, wie g in Genie, j in Journal: *azure* ['æʒə], *jazz* [dʒæz], *jeep* [dʒiːp], *large* [lɑːdʒ].

[ʃ] stimmloses sch, wie im Deutschen Schnee, rasch: *shake* [ʃeɪk], *washing* ['wɒʃɪŋ], *lash* [læʃ].

[θ] im Deutschen nicht vorhandener stimmloser Lispellaut; durch Anlegen der Zunge an die oberen Schneidezähne hervorgebracht: *thin* [θɪn], *path* [pɑːθ], *method* ['meθəd].

[ð] derselbe Laut stimmhaft, d.h. mit Stimmton: *there* [ðeə], *breathe* [briːð], *father* ['fɑːðə].

[s] stimmloser Zischlaut, entsprechend dem deutschen ß in Spaß, reißen: *see* [siː], *hats* [hæts], *decide* [dɪ'saɪd].

[z] stimmhafter Zischlaut wie im Deutschen sausen: *zeal* [ziːl], *rise* [raɪz], *horizon* [hə'raɪzn].

[ŋ] wird wie der deutsche Nasenlaut in fangen, singen gebildet: *ring* [rɪŋ], *singer* ['sɪŋə].

[ŋk] derselbe Laut mit nachfolgendem k wie im Deutschen senken, Wink: *ink* [ɪŋk], *tinker* ['tɪŋkə].

[w] flüchtiges, mit Lippe an Lippe gesprochenes w, aus der Mundstellung für uː gebildet: *will* [wɪl], *swear* [sweə], *queen* [kwiːn].

[f] stimmloser Lippenlaut wie im Deutschen flott: *fat* [fæt], *tough* [tʌf], *effort* ['efət].

[v] stimmhafter Lippenlaut wie im Deutschen Vase, Ventil: *vein* [veɪn], *velvet* ['velvɪt].

[j] flüchtiger zwischen j und i schwebender Laut: *onion* ['ʌnjən], *yes* [jes], *filial* ['fɪljəl].

Verwendete Abkürzungen

A.D.	anno Domini (= nach Christus)
AE	amerikanisches Englisch
A.M.	ante meridiem (= vormittags)
BE	britisches Englisch
coll.	colloquial (= umgangssprachlich)
e-m	einem
e-r	einer
etw.	etwas
Frz.	Französisch
i.e.	id est (= das heißt)
j-n	jemanden
Lat.	Lateinisch
o.s.	oneself
o.'s	one's
P.M.	post meridiem (= nachmittags)
Pret.	preterite (= Vergangenheit)
sl.	Slang
s.o.	someone
s.th.	something
Sup.	Superlativ

A Mighty Nice Man

The child Charlotte sat on the narrow **curbstone**, her cheek against one knee, drawing **idly** in the dust with a stick. She **sniffed** at the flesh of her leg, smelt the dust and the sweat on it. Then she sighed and threw away the stick.

"Em'lie," she said.

Emilie, age nine, was standing behind her, with her back against the sun-warm wooden post, her toes **braced** on the edge of the sidewalk.

"Huh?" Emilie breathed.

"Play like I've got a store. Play like I've got a grocer store an' you've gotta buy **stuff**… . Huh, Em'lie?"

Emilie was so **bored** and sleepy she did not reply. Her gray **sullen** eyes looked out across the road and the whole scene was yellow to her, the dirt of the road, the **squatting** house just beyond, the dry fields: yellow pulsing heat and silence.

"Em'lie! You crazy? … Answer me!" Charlotte turned around on the curb and **glowered at** her.

"Wha'?" said Emilie, and pushed herself away from the post.

"I've gotta store an' you must buy stuff." She reached for the tiny red **truck** that was their common **property** and began filling it with **pebbles**. "An' then I must **deliver** it. You gotta go home first an' then you must telephone." She **clutched** the truck in one dirty hand as she **scowled at** Emilie.

They heard footsteps in the **grit** of the road. Charlotte forgot her game and they both looked up the **slope**. Emilie

---

mighty nice [ˌmaɪtɪ 'naɪs] supernett **curbstone** ['kɜːbstəʊn] Randstein **idly** ['aɪdlɪ] faul, träge **to sniff** [snɪf] riechen, schnüffeln **to brace** [breɪs] klammern **stuff** [stʌf] Zeug **bored** [bɔːd] gelangweilt **sullen** ['sʌlən] mürrisch **squatting** ['skwɒtɪŋ] kauernd **to glower at s.o.** ['glaʊə] j-n finster anblicken **truck** [trʌk] Lastwagen **property** ['prɒpətɪ] Eigentum **pebble** ['pebl] Kieselstein **to deliver** [dɪ'lɪvə] liefern **to clutch** [klʌtʃ] fest umklammern **to scowl at s.o.** [skaʊl] j-n düster anblicken **grit** [grɪt] Kies, Sand **slope** [sləʊp] Hang

brushed the **mottled** blond hair out of her eyes and **squinted**. **Her** left **eye was cast**, and she twisted up that side of her face whenever she looked at anything.

"I **betcha** it's a **boarder** from Mrs. Osterman's," Charlotte said. "I betcha he's from New York, too."

He turned onto the sidewalk that began half a block from Charlotte's house. Emilie could see him now, a short figure in **unpressed** white trousers. He saw them, too, and began **whistling** a tune.

"Hello," he said, taking in both of them.

"H'lo," they replied **in unison**.

He stopped a minute, looked about him. "Gonna be here when I get back?" He spoke quietly, smiling. "I'll bring you some **candy**."

Charlotte and Emilie **surveyed** him silently.

"I like ... I like *any* kind of candy," Charlotte told him.

He laughed, **winked at** them and walked on down the sidewalk. Once he turned and waved, but only Charlotte saw that. They were both **motionless** a long time, watching.

"**Reckon** he'll come back, Em'lie?"

"Huh?"

"Reckon he'll come back this way?"

"Huh?"

"I **sed** ... reckon he'll come *back?*"

But Emilie moved off without a word toward her house and Charlotte sat on the curb, resting her face against one knee as she traced in the dust. Soon the **screen door** to Emilie's house

---

mottled ['mɒtld] gefleckt **to squint** [skwɪnt] die Augen zusammenkneifen **her eye was cast** [aɪ, kɑːst] sie hatte einen Augenfehler **I betcha** *sl. i.e.* **I bet you** ['betʃə] 'ich wette mit dir' **boarder** ['bɔːdə] (Unter-)Mieter **unpressed** [ʌn'prest] ungebügelt **to whistle** ['wɪsl] Pfeifen **in unison** ['juːnɪsn] gleichzeitig, im gleichen Tonfall **candy** ['kændɪ] Süßigkeiten **to survey s.o.** [sə'veɪ] j-n mustern **to wink at s.o.** [wɪŋk] j-m winken **motionless** ['məʊʃnləs] reglos **'reckon ...?** *sl. i.e.* **'do you ...?'** ['rekən] 'glaubst du ...?' **sed** *sl. i.e.* **said** [sed] **screen door** ['skriːn dɔː] Fliegengittertür

screeched, closed with a double **slap**, and Emilie's bare **heels thudded** across the **porch**.

"Huh," said Emilie, and handed Charlotte a small pale **peach**. Charlotte took it silently, bit into the fruit with darkish baby teeth.

"Betcha that man's got a car."

"Huh?"

"I sed"—she took a deep breath—"I betcha that man's got a *ca-ar.*"

"Wha' man?"

"That *ma-an* ... what just passed."

Emilie licked her peach-**stained** fingers. "He ain't comin' back." She sighed, looked across the hot road to the **blurry** yellowish fields. The **bugs** in the grass, in the trees, were singing rhythmically. Two clicks and a long buzz. Down the road where it met the street that led into town they heard Mr. Wynecoop's **station wagon**. They knew it from all the other cars in the neighborhood. Charlotte and Emilie sat on the edge of the curb and looked.

As he passed, Mr. Wynecoop waved a stiff-fingered hand at them, and they **chanted**, "H'lo, ol' man Wynecoop."

The car pulled up the hill, reached the top, sighed as it hit level ground. Charlotte kept watching for the man in white. She stood up once and looked toward town, but the view was mostly shut out by the trees along the sidewalk.

Emilie **smirked** and grunted **contemptuously**.

Charlotte held the empty truck in one hand and stared down the walk. "*You* **cou'nt** see him if he *was* comin'." Sud-

---

to screech [skriːtʃ] quietschen **slap** [slæp] Schlag **heel** [hiːl] Ferse **to thud** [θʌd] *hier:* stapfen **porch** [pɔːtʃ] Veranda **peach** [piːtʃ] Pfirsich **stained** [steɪnd] schmutzig, klebrig **blurry** ['blɜːrɪ] unscharf, verschwommen **bug** [bʌg] Insekt **station wagon** ['steɪʃn ˌwægən] Kombiwagen **to chant** [tʃɑːnt] (herunter-)leiern **to smirk** [smɜːk] grinsen **contemptuously** [kən'temptjʊəslɪ] verächtlich **coun't** *sl. i.e.* **couldn't** [kʊnt]

denly she drew in her breath. "He's comin', all right," she whispered, and ran **stooping** over to Emilie by the curb. She began stabbing in the dust, her heart beating fast.

Then Emilie heard his footsteps and twisted around and peered into the yellowness. He was whistling again. The blur of white came closer.

"He's got candy!" Charlotte said.

The man took his cigarette out of his mouth and threw it down.

"Hello," he said quietly, then glanced at the houses and back at the two little girls on the curb. He handed the bag to Charlotte. Two **licorice** sticks stuck out of the top, and she was disappointed to see that it was all **penny candy**, **unwrapped** caramels and sugar hearts that sell five for a cent. Once an old man from Mrs. Osterman's had brought her five-cent **candy bars**.

Slowly she put one end of a licorice stick into her mouth. The man **shuffled** uneasily, leaned against a tree and lighted another cigarette. "You didn't tell me your name," he said finally.

She told him, and he said his name was Robbie.

"I've got a car… . Want to go riding sometime?" He kept shifting and taking his hands in and out of his pockets. "I bet you like riding, Charlotte."

"I sure do," she said, and a dark stream of licorice **juice** ran down her chin.

The man leaning against the tree sprang toward her, drew a **wadded handkerchief** out of his hip pocket. He put one hand back of her head and wiped her face hard. "You're …

---

to stoop [stuːp] sich bücken **licorice** ['lɪkərɪʃ] Lakritze **penny candy** ['penɪ ˌkændɪ] billige Süßigkeiten **unwrapped** [ʌn'ræpt] nicht eingewickelt **candy bar** ['kændɪ bɑː] Schokoriegel **to shuffle** ['ʃʌfl] hin- und herrutschen **juice** [dʒuːs] Saft **wadded** ['wɒdɪd] zusammengeknüllt **handkerchief** ['hæŋkətʃɪf] Taschentuch

pretty **messy**." Then he stood up again and put the handkerchief back. Emilie was watching him steadily, curiously. He felt the **hostility** in her twisted mouth.

He drew **viciously** on his cigarette. "How'd you like to go riding this evening?" he whispered. "After dinner."

"I'd like that," Charlotte said.

Then he went off quietly, looking back at them, smiling and friendly.

Charlotte was **proud** of herself. She leaned back on her hands and the thin muscles in her **thighs** showed under the dirt-streaked skin.

"He didn't ask *you* to go."

Emilie sighed. "He ain't comin'. You wait an' see."

So Charlotte waited. She finished the candy alone, picked at her noon meal, and **brooded** happily in the shade of the house, humming to herself. Then she lay in the **patched-up hammock** on her front porch and looked at the pictures in a **frayed** funny paper book. The afternoon was hot and long and silent.

After supper Charlotte went out to the road and stood by the tree. Her mother had **given her a sponge bath**, and she had a cotton dress on instead of the thin **romper suit** she wore all day. She had told her mother nothing about the man from Mrs. Osterman's. The fast-setting sun sent hot horizontal **rays** into her face. She was sure he would come. She tried to picture the car, like the ones she had seen in the movies. That was the kind of car *he* would have. And she would step into the big front seat and they would drive away with hardly a sound. They would drive fast.

---

messy ['mesɪ] schmutzig **hostility** [hɒ'stɪlətɪ] Feindseligkeit **viciously** ['vɪʃəslɪ] heftig **proud** [praʊd] stolz **thigh** [θaɪ] Oberschenkel **to brood** [bru:d] brüten, nachdenken **patched-up** [ˌpætʃt'ʌp] geflickt **hammock** ['hæmək] Hängematte **frayed** [freɪd] abgegriffen **to give s.o. a sponge bath** ['spʌndʒ bɑ:θ] j-n mit e-m Schwamm abwaschen **romper suit** ['rɒmpə su:t] Spielanzug (für Kleinkinder) **ray** [reɪ] Strahl

But after a while she got tired and came in to the front porch. The wood was hot to her bare feet. She leaned on one side of the hammock, pushed herself into it. Still she listened and there was no sound of a car. Then the screen door to Emilie's house shrieked, stopped and shrieked again. Emilie appeared, unwashed and **tousled**, eating the remains of a slice of bread and butter. She came **deliberately** onto Charlotte's porch, stood chewing **reflectively** as she stared at her in the hammock. Charlotte **disdained** to look at her.

"Oh ... *he* ain't comin'," she said, and turned around and walked to the steps. She heard something down the walk. "That your mother comin'? *She* don't know, I betcha."

Charlotte **bounced** out of the hammock. "Listen, Em'lie ..." She **frowned** furiously. "If you ... if you say to her ..." She **clenched her fists** at her sides and Emilie gazed at her **solemnly**.

"Huh!"

But Charlotte had won.

There was no more sun, but it was still light. Charlotte's mother came back from the store. None of them said a word. The woman went into the house and Charlotte could hear her drawing water for the baby. Finally Emilie went **hop-skipping** across the front yard, into her house.

Charlotte lay in the hammock and listened for him. Someone was walking, whistling. She ran down to the sidewalk and saw him coming. He was dressed in white again with his jacket unbuttoned. He stopped when he saw her, smiled and **beckoned**. And she glanced once at her house, then ran up the warm pavement to where he stood.

"Where's your car?"

---

tousled ['taʊzld] zerzaust **deliberately** [dɪ'lɪbərətlɪ] mit e-r bestimmten Absicht **reflectively** [rɪ'flektɪvlɪ] nachdenklich **to disdain** [dɪs'deɪn] verschmähen **to bounce** [baʊns] springen **to frown** [fraʊn] die Stirne runzeln **to clench o.'s fists** [ˌklentʃ ... 'fɪsts] die Fäuste ballen **solemnly** ['sɒləmlɪ] ernst(haft) **hop-skipping** ['hɒpˌskɪpɪŋ] auf e-m Bein hüpfend **to beckon** ['bekən] heranwinken

He looked about him, grinned and **jerked** his head. "Up the road… . We don't want nobody to know. You didn't tell nobody, did you?"

"No."

They walked together. She could hardly keep up with him, so he took her hand. The fields opened up on either side after the pavement stopped. Charlotte strained up to see the car, and then the road turned suddenly and they came upon it parked by the roadside. It was big, but not so bright as those in the movies. He opened the door and lifted her in, her feet **dangling** over the edge of the seat. Then he came in from the other side.

"All set?"

"Uh-huh." Charlotte was looking at the car inside.

"Like it?" he asked, and wiped his nose on the back of his hand.

They didn't drive off immediately. Charlotte was examining the **gaudily colored dashboard**, its clock with green numbers and silver hands. The other circles she did not understand, but they were all beautiful, colored and shining. The man caught her hand suddenly and she felt his fingers warm and **moist**, felt her mouth twist up as though she were about to cry. Then she wished that she had not come, wished that she were back on the front porch with Emilie. But he was smiling, laughing, even, as he started the car.

"You like to go fast?"

Charlotte tried to answer, but her lips were stiff. He **squeezed** her hand again.

"I like a lot of speed."

Then through the engine's noise she heard someone calling

---

to jerk [dʒɜːk] eine ruckartige Bewegung machen **to dangle** ['dæŋgl] baumeln **gaudily colored** ['gɔːdɪlɪ 'kʌləd] auffällig bunt **dashboard** ['dæʃbɔːd] Armaturenbrett **moist** [mɔɪst] feucht **to squeeze** [skwiːz] fest drücken

her name. The man heard it, too, and **released** her hand. But the car was moving on toward her house.

"Charlotte! Charlo-otte!"

"That's my mother," Charlotte said quietly.

Charlotte noticed that he frowned and that his hands **tightened** on the **steering wheel**. She felt the cool breeze in her face and she wanted to go on riding, but they were not going fast and she wanted to go fast. As they came near the house, she pressed herself against the seat, hoping her mother would not see her.

The woman stood with one foot on the curb, her **apron** hanging almost to the ground. She waved at them and he slowed the car. She came nearer, hiding her hands under her apron.

"Charlotte." She grinned, but she looked at the man almost flirtatiously. "Em'lie said you were out ridin'. I just wanted to make sure where you was ... an' I need you to help with the baby now." She pushed some strands of hair behind her ear.

The man at the wheel smiled broadly and said, "How d'you do?"

Charlotte's mother nodded to him. "I **allus** have Charlotte help me with the baby 'bout this time after supper... . It's awful nice o' you to take her out ridin', mister, but she didn't say nothin' to me about it." She laughed nervously.

"Sure, I know," he said. He stretched one arm across and opened the door gallantly. "Maybe tomorrow, then. I'll be around for a few days."

The woman looked **in awe** at the shiny **dials** and **knobs**, the **upholstered** seats. "Why ... I'd like you to take her ridin' ... most anytime."

Then Charlotte and her mother walked hand in hand down

---

to release [rɪ'liːs] loslassen **to tighten** ['taɪtn] eng umklammern **steering wheel** ['stɪərɪŋ wiːl] Steuerrad **apron** ['eɪprən] Schürze **allus** *sl. i.e.* **always** ['ɑːləs] **in awe** [ɔː] voller Ehrfurcht **dial** ['daɪəl] (Instrumenten-)Anzeige **knob** [nɒb] Knopf, Hebel **upholstered** [ʌp'həʊlstəd] gepolstert

the sidewalk. Once the woman cast a **timid glance** back at the car. "He's a mighty nice man for a city **fellah**, Charlotte. Where'd you meet up with him? ... An' say, ain't that a pretty car?"

Charlotte watched the ground pass below her bare feet. Her free hand brushed along the **coarse** grass that grew high.

"Maybe he'll be around tomorrow," her mother said.

One blade of grass Charlotte caught **convulsively** and the edges jerked through her fingers. As she looked at her **thumb**, two thin red lines came out of the flesh.

---

timid ['tɪmɪd] ängstlich, scheu **glance** [glɑːns] Blick **fellah** *sl. i.e.* **fellow** ['felə] Kerl, Typ **coarse** [kɔːs] rau **convulsively** [kən'vʌlsɪvlɪ] krampfhaft **thumb** [θʌm] Daumen

The Hollow Oracle

The black mass of the house sprang out of the darkness, and he **tripped** on the wooden step. He knocked on the **screen-door frame**, **seized** the **knob** and **wrenched** it back and forth as though he must be let in before a **pursuer** overtook him. Like a murderer he held the powerful **clawhammer** straight down at his side, in a grip that made the hammer a part of his arm, **welded** in the ache of his muscles. He shook the door until the sound grew crazy in the silence, and he stopped, losing then the **momentum** that had carried him the two miles down the road, the murderer's momentum that had started twenty minutes before, like the beginning of the act itself. In the stillness there was time to hear his own **gasping** breath, to feel the eyes in the dark behind him. He pressed close to the house, making no sound.

The door pushed against him. He stepped back, his arm shooting up at an **awkward angle**, like a girl's arm about to throw a stone. But it was several seconds before he could distinguish her figure on the **threshold**, and her head was inches higher than his hand. His arm dropped slowly, **indecisively**.

Then the woman said, "Arthur? ... It's you, Arthur! Come in!" Her voice was hollow in the house, coming from nowhere.

He **hesitated**, almost turned and fled, but now he feared the night through which he had just come even more than the house. He came in quickly, and in the movement lost her figure in the **porch**. The **stale**, yellowish smell of the house

---

hollow ['hɒləʊ] hohl **to trip** [trɪp] stolpern **screen-door** ['skriːndɔː] Fliegengittertür **frame** [freɪm] Rahmen **to seize** [siːz] ergreifen **knob** [nɒb] Türknauf **to wrench s.th.** [rentʃ] an etw. rütteln **pursuer** [pə'sjuːə] Verfolger **clawhammer** ['klɔːhæmə] Klauenhammer **welded** ['weldɪd] verschweißt **momentum** [məʊ'mentəm] Impuls **gasping** ['gɑːspɪŋ] keuchend **awkward** ['ɔːkwəd] ungünstig **angle** ['æŋgl] Winkel **threshold** ['θreʃhəʊld] (Tür-)Schwelle **indecisively** [ˌɪndɪ'saɪsɪvlɪ] unentschlossen **to hesitate** ['hezɪteɪt] zögern **porch** [pɔːtʃ] Veranda **stale** [steɪl] schal

invaded him, lifeless, **insidious**, forcing upon his mind a thousand visits with her. He **crouched**, breathing shallowly, watching for the woman, who could see him well in the dark.

"I guess it's been all of three weeks since you've come to see me, Arthur."

He said nothing. It had been four months. Almost exactly four months. He **cursed himself** for remembering now. By now it should have been done! But how could he see her without some light? It would be horrible to miss with the hammer. And yet he wished it might be done without seeing her.

"Come into the kitchen and I'll fix some tea." She glided away from him, and he heard her long cotton skirt **rustling** faintly over the **bare** floor.

He came after her, **avoiding** by old knowledge the porch furniture. "Before the lamp is lit!" he swore. "Before I can really see her!" But he had sworn to the night air, swinging his hammer like **Thor** in the unresisting air, that he would strike her before she could recognize him, and he had failed. He felt like a diver who has looked too long at the water to make the **leap**.

The kitchen was large, and he did not find her until the lamp **waxed** suddenly and filled the place with golden light.

He saw it then. He stared long seconds at the **distortion** of her figure, stared with his **myopic** eyes wide in their dark **sockets**, his thin lips parted in an expression that was strange to his **tense** face. He watched her until he grew conscious of a kind of hypnosis over himself, a feeling of **giddiness** and **exhaustion**. He hid the hammer behind his trouser leg and backed against the sideboard.

---

insidious [ɪn'sɪdɪəs] heimtückisch **to crouch** [kraʊtʃ] sich ducken **to curse o.s.** [kɜːs] sich verfluchen **rustling** ['rʌslɪŋ] raschelnd **bare** [beə] bloß, blank **to avoid** [ə'vɔɪd] vermeiden **Thor** [θɔː] *nordischer Gott des Donners* **leap** [liːp] Sprung **to wax** [wæks] zunehmen, stärker werden (Licht etc.) **distortion** [dɪ'stɔːʃn] Verzerrung, Veränderung der Form **myopic** [maɪ'ɒpɪk] kurzsichtig **socket** ['sɒkɪt] *hier:* Augenhöhle **tense** [tens] angespannt **giddiness** ['gɪdɪnəs] Schwindel **exhaustion** [ɪg'zɔːstʃn] Erschöpfung

Emma did not once look at him. She filled the kettle, struck a match to the gas burner. She moved gracefully, weightlessly, in spite of the **bulk** of her body. A few gray hairs, escaped from the **mottle-brown comb**, caught the lamplight like a **halo** about her smallish head. Her hands, for all their activity, made gentle, uncertain movements. But there was, even in the placing of the lid on the teakettle, an expression of a **generous** and **indiscriminating** love.

The man watching her grew afraid. It was the child he was afraid of, not of Emma. It had invested her with a reality that bewildered him and **stupefied** him. He began to feel that his **inertia** was willed by Emma, and by the subtle aroma of the house. To strengthen himself he whispered, "It is **inevitable**! … Inevitable!"

As though the words had reminded her he stood there, she turned to him and said, "You must have a great deal to tell me, Arthur, after three weeks."

The **trite**, **courteous** words embarrassed him. She was not herself, he thought. But what was herself? Her **rapt** attention when they read together? The fascination when he talked about the creations of his brain? The **intent** of his paintings that he could never put on **canvas**? He cleared his throat. "No, I …"

"About what you've been painting, and thinking and reading, about the walks in the woods, and the long nights walking," Emma went on. She stood now in the center of the kitchen, facing him, **pale** and calm. Her eyes, clear as a young girl's, played without direction about his face like blue **mists**.

"I haven't painted at all," he said. He noticed a kind of sat-

---

bulk [bʌlk] Schwere, Größe **mottle-brown** [ˌmɒtl'braʊn] braun gefleckt **comb** [kəʊm] Kamm, Haarspange **halo** ['heɪləʊ] Heiligenschein **generous** ['dʒenrəs] großzügig **indiscriminating** [ˌɪndɪ'skrɪmɪneɪtɪŋ] unterschiedslos **to stupefy s.o.** ['stjuːpɪfaɪ] j-n vor den Kopf stoßen **inertia** [ɪ'nɜːʃə] Trägheit **inevitable** [ɪn'evɪtəbl] unvermeidlich **trite** [traɪt] platt, banal **courteous** ['kɜːtɪəs] höflich **rapt** [ræpt] gebannt **intent** [ɪn'tent] Absicht, Ziel **canvas** ['kænvəs] (Mal-) Leinwand **pale** [peɪl] blass **mist** [mɪst] Nebel, Dunst

isfaction in her, a childlike **pride**, and he wondered if she were waiting for him to mention the child. The thought **disgusted** him.

"It is not fit for you to create while the child is being created," Emma said.

A sickening **thrill** went through him.

She came straight toward him, and he slipped aside. She took down the white **china** cups and saucers from the cabinet over the sideboard. "The air is filled with creation," she remarked.

He recognized with sudden **shame** that the words were precisely his, that he had said them one night as they stood by the **well** in the garden. To what **exultation** had he given voice that night?

"I have told the people again and again that my child is God-given, and how few will believe," she continued, without passion, with only a **conviction** that flowed like a thin, buried stream in her. "So it has been since the days of Sarah."

He gripped the hammer, but his energy was from shame, **wasting** itself in the **trembling** of his fingers. Now he was far from striking her, so far that he did not think to ask himself why he **delayed**. Her voice like the wind, **void** and **capricious**, rose and fell, parroting the words, enchanting him. *Sarah … and the creation of the world … and the days of Sarah …*

Still she stood, holding the cups and saucers in her long hands upturned before her. "You have always understood such things, Arthur… . You can understand why it is my duty to speak God's word on the streets."

---

pride [praɪd] Stolz **to disgust s.o.** [dɪs'gʌst] j-n abstoßen **thrill** [θrɪl] Erregung, Anspannung **china** ['tʃaɪnə] Porzellan **shame** [ʃeɪm] Scham, Schmach **well** [wel] Brunnen **exultation** [ˌegzʌl'teɪʃn] Jubel, Frohlocken **conviction** [kən'vɪkʃn] Überzeugung **to waste** [weɪst] vergeuden **trembling** ['tremblɪŋ] Zittern **to delay** [dɪ'leɪ] zögern **void** [vɔɪd] leer **capricious** [kə'prɪʃəs] launisch, launenhaft

He said nothing. He drew his upper lip between his teeth, seeking among many remembered conversations the pieces that had built the **precarious** structure of her belief.

"You yourself have told me that those of God's inspiration should **proclaim** themselves. I shall tell every living soul unto my last breath and they will believe finally."

"Oh, hush! Hush!" He stepped forward, but he could not have brought himself to touch her. He **glanced** behind him at the window, but the **squares** reflected only the scene in the kitchen, the man and the woman with the golden lamp between them. He looked at it for several seconds, wondering at the strange sensation he had of not **participating** in the action in the room.

"They do believe," Emma continued quietly. "Some have come to me and bowed down and said they believe ... and the others ... they believe, too. That's why they want me to go away... . They would make my child of **mortal** man. Their hearts are closed to the spirit and their eyes bent down to the earth!"

His words! His words, all of them, come back to fill him with shame. His **lean** face, **sloping back** from the **finlike** nose, **thrust forward**, parting the mystic **veils** around her.

"They were here today... . What did they say?" And at the same time, he was thinking, what did it matter what they said? Or what did it matter if they knew, since he had come to kill her?

Emma turned her face to the ceiling, closed her eyes. "They said we are mortal men, and we proclaim our blindness. We proclaim our need to be saved."

"I mean Roy ... Roy's men, Emma. The men from the **courthouse**. What did they say?"

---

precarious [prɪ'keərɪəs] unsicher, fragwürdig **to proclaim o.s.** [prə'kleɪm] sich offenbaren, (s-n Glauben) kundtun **to glance** [glɑːns] e-n Blick werfen **square** [skweə] (Glas-)Viereck **to participate** [pɑː'tɪsɪpeɪt] teilnehmen **mortal** ['mɔːtl] sterblich **lean** [liːn] mager, hager **to slope back** [ˌsləʊp 'bæk] abfallen, zurückspringen **finlike** ['fɪnlaɪk] *hier:* scharf geschnitten **to thrust forward** [ˌθrʌst 'fɔːwəd] nach vorne schnellen **veil** [veɪl] Schleier **courthouse** ['kɔːthaʊs] Ge-

"The twelve men did come and they said we are humble men before you and there is a **beam in our eye**!"

He seized her arm and a cup fell at their feet, breaking like an eggshell. Emma started. "No! What did they say, Emma! What!" he whispered as desperately as though the answer would free him.

She frowned, looked down on the **shards** at her feet, confused at the disorder. "They said I must leave the town unless I tell who the man was," she sighed.

He took his hand away. Her words were so clear, he felt suddenly she had been **pretending** the rest. "But you know there was no man," he said, and the sentence was supplied from some part of his brain that wanted him to live and be saved.

"I said, 'Ask for him and no man will show himself, for there was none.'"

His shoulders relaxed. How sweet would it be to believe! To sit and talk and drink tea and to go home believing, and thinking happily as he walked home of all the **multitude** of things in the world that he loved and which gave him pleasure.

"They have asked," he whispered, "and you are right, there was no one."

"Oh, no." Emma smiled. "Yes, it is **divine**. It will be a divine child."

She turned her face toward him, waiting for more beautiful words from his lips, trusting him, and tasting joy in each **syllable**. But he could not open his mouth. He could think of no beautiful words. "What else did they say, Emma? Do you remember?"

She looked at him, with the **suggestion** of disappointment in the movement of the eyebrows that lay pale and fine below

---

richtsgebäude **beam in one's eye** [biːm] der Balken im eigenen Auge *(Bibl. u. fig.)* **shard** [ʃɑːd] Splitter **to pretend** [prɪˈtend] vortäuschen **multitude** [ˈmʌltɪtjuːd] Vielzahl **divine** [dɪˈvaɪn] göttlich **syllable** [ˈsɪləbl] Silbe **suggestion** [səˈdʒestʃn] Andeutung

the handsome forehead. "They said people think it was the Negro Jim Crawford and they'd have to lynch him."

The **weight** of his **guilt** lifted suddenly. His head was light. The waters flowed away, into this new channel, where he saw them swirling, catching up another creature. He did not participate. The **maelstrom** had passed over him. "Lynch him! ... Will they lynch him? When will they lynch him!"

Emma went into the dining room and set the dishes down on the table, arranging them. "They didn't say."

The flatness of her voice brought him back to his senses. They had told Emma they would lynch the Negro in order that she, **in pity**, might tell the truth. They didn't think the Negro guilty. Why should they **suspect** a man who was fifty years old? Who **tended** his farm by himself and went to church on Sundays? Emma did not realize what she was saying! She was repeating words!

She came back and turned off the gas, poured the water into the teapot, lifting the kettle with difficulty.

"Yes, they should lynch him," he said, **confusedly**, "and get it off their minds."

"It would be but one more sin to be **redeemed**," she replied.

Then, as if the words first took meaning for her, she shook her head.

"Oh, no, Arthur... . Oh, no, I don't understand you tonight. I'm sure I don't."

"I mean they will never understand such things as this. They must have **blood revenge**, and only then will they stop **annoying** you." And he felt he was two people, one talking about the other, because certainly the blood revenge would be himself.

---

weight [weɪt] Gewicht **guilt** [gɪlt] Schuld **maelstrom** ['meɪlstrɒm] Strudel, Sog **in pity** ['pɪtɪ] aus Mitleid **to suspect** [sə'spekt] verdächtigen **to tend** [tend] versorgen, sich kümmern um **confusedly** [kən'fjuːzɪdlɪ] verwirrt **to redeem** [rɪ'diːm] abbüßen, wieder gutmachen **blood revenge** [ˌblʌd rɪ'vendʒ] Blutrache **to annoy s.o.** [ə'nɔɪ] j-n belästigen

"They are only children, **clamoring for** the answer." She took the potholder from the nail by the stove and set the white and gold teapot on it. She went into the dining room. "But they may well lynch him, **in spite of** all that I say to save him."

"How do you know?"

"Does God save the **innocent** from their **pain**? The sins must mount up against the guilty... ."

"Did Roy Patterson say they'd definitely lynch him?"

"Oh, no." Emma came back and hung up the potholder. "But Jim Crawford says it was you. He says he's seen you here so much at night."

The blood **drained** from him, downward to his feet and away, leaving him empty and floating to nowhere. "When—when did he say that?"

"Today. He was here today with the others." Emma got some tea **buns** from the **larder** and arranged them on a plate.

"But he only says that to save himself! Anyone can see that!"

"Yes," Emma replied. "That's why I think they will kill him."

"Who thinks it was I? Who!" He **strode** to her place at the table, where she sat calmly preparing her cup of tea, the gray head bent delicately, the hands busy.

"Come have your tea, Arthur, while it's hot."

"But who? ... Who believes?"

She did not even look at him. "Arthur, I don't understand you tonight."

"How is it the Negro saw me come here?" he flung at her. "He **spied on** us! He spies on us!"

He laughed, but **choked with** fear. "Everybody knows I

---

to clamor for s.th. ['klæmə] etw. lautstark verlangen **in spite of** [spaɪt] trotz **innocent** ['ɪnəsnt] Unschuldige(r) **pain** [peɪn] Schmerz **to drain** [dreɪn] ablaufen, leer werden **bun** [bʌn] süßes Brötchen **larder** ['lɑːdə] Speisekammer **strode** *Pret.* **to stride** [strəʊd, straɪd] schreiten **to spy on s.o.** [spaɪ] j-n bespitzeln **to choke with s.th.** [tʃəʊk] an etw. ersticken

come here to see you," he whispered. "It's no secret, is it? And nobody but Jim Crawford says it was I… . Isn't it so?"

Emma was silent. Then, "Oh, I don't understand you, Arthur!"

He seized her by the shoulders, turned her toward him. "You understand. Say it! … You know it wasn't I! … Say it, Emma!"

"What wasn't you?"

He relaxed. He wanted to laugh again, wildly to fall into tears, to **throttle** her, to embrace her. He stood straight and tense. "It wasn't! It wasn't!" he screamed. "No, it wasn't." The hammer **clattered** to the floor.

Emma looked at him, **uncomprehending**.

The escape of the hammer from his hand **sobered** him all at once. Neither of them looked at it, lying on the floor at his feet. Emma had observed it. Her eyes were gentle. How delicate was the balance of her belief! he thought. He calmed himself **deliberately**. He must not touch those precariously balanced **scales** behind her eyes… . If the Negro were lynched, the town would stop its questionings, the **alms** of the town would still be given, the suspicions on himself would pass away… . Emma would have the child … but if the child were alive! How could Emma give birth to a live thing? … And suppose the strange processes in her mind one day reassembled the facts and she were to announce them in the church as she had announced her visitation from the angel of God!

The **torment** seized him once more and he wondered that he had felt those few seconds of freedom. "There is no solution but that the Negro child should die," he said. "I'll see that he does. I'll fix it."

But Emma wasn't listening. She broke a **cinnamon** bun in

---

to throttle s.o. ['θrɒtl] j-n erdrosseln **to clatter** ['klætə] scheppern **uncomprehending** [ʌnˌkɒmprɪ'hendɪŋ] verständnislos **to sober s.o.** ['səʊbə] j-n ernüchtern, wieder zur Vernunft bringen **deliberately** [dɪ'lɪbərətlɪ] absichtlich, bewusst **scale** [skeɪl] Waagschale **alms** [ɑːmz] Almosen **torment** ['tɔːmənt] Qual **cinnamon** ['sɪnəmən] Zimt

half, ate it slowly, dipping portions of it into her tea, turning her smooth, pale face slightly as she took her bites.

Strangely she grew more and more real. She was no longer something **artificial**, without past or future. The child was a promise of some tomorrow. She was no longer like one of his **blank** canvases, on which he would paint what he would. She was real. One day she would remember, and speak the truth.

She rose up. "I want to go into the garden. I want to go and talk." She went into the kitchen and turned, waiting for him.

The lamplight put a ring about her head. She was like an angel, transparent, without understanding of **deception**.

"There is no solution but that he must die!" he repeated.

Emma waited. "I don't understand you. I don't understand what troubles you."

"It wasn't I!" he cried, as if he must fight her **accusation**. "No one can think it was I when they know how I take care of her. Everyone knows I take care of her like a child! That I treat her better than any other man would... . Everyone knows what she means to me ... alone in that house!" He came close to her, **pleading** to the hollow oracle. "They know how I feed her and talk to her just as though she could hear me, when any other man would have put her into an **institution**! Didn't they all say I should put her away or I'd go crazy? Don't they all say what a rare good man I am to keep her? Don't they, Emma?"

"Of course, that's so."

He laughed bitter, **falsetto**. "I guess Jim Crawford ... I guess they'll all be surprised to know how we read Blake and Shelley and drink tea and look at paintings and talk about things no one else can understand! ... I guess they'd be surprised to know that's all we do, wouldn't they, Emma, my darling?"

---

artificial [ˌɑːtɪˈfɪʃl] künstlich **blank** [blæŋk] leer **deception** [dɪˈsepʃn] Täuschung **accusation** [ˌækjuːˈzeɪʃn] Anklage **pleading** [ˈpliːdɪŋ] inständig bittend **institution** [ˌɪnstɪˈtjuːʃn] *hier:* Pflegeheim **falsetto** [fɔːlˈsetəʊ] mit e-r Fistelstimme

"Oh, yes ... yes."

"Isn't it so they call me 'professor'?"

"That's so," Emma replied. And, bored with his **tumultuous moods**, she turned and continued on her way to the back door.

He followed her, heard the faint rustle of her long dress, the **click** of the door **latch**. When Emma went out, he stood on the threshold, listening to hear if anyone was waiting outside.

He stepped down after a moment, hurried after her, and whispered fearfully, "I must go, Emma. I'll be going now!" He was feeble and **insignificant** in the **expanse** of the night. But a voice inside him countered, *Where? Where?*

They passed through the **grape arbor**, whose white **trellises** showed **occasionally** through the leaves. Emma was somewhere near him, **amorphous**, escaping him. He longed for the security of the hammer in his hand. He turned quickly to go back for it, and then he was afraid to enter the house alone.

"It was here I heard the voice," Emma said, leaning back against the post that supported the well roof. "It said, so quietly I could hardly hear, that from this small village my child should **cast** a **beam** so fine and strong it would encircle the earth."

He remembered when he had said "from that small village ..." and what had he said would encircle the earth?

"Wherever men's hearts are closed against one another, they should be opened to see all the workings of the earth and of themselves as a **reflection** of God's glory ... all the music, poetry, painting, all creations would be **delights doing honor to** God. All powers of mind and spirit **derived from** God."

---

tumultuous [tjuː'mʌltjʊəs] heftig **mood** [muːd] Stimmung, Laune **click** [klɪk] Schnappen **latch** [lætʃ] Riegel **insignificant** [ˌɪnsɪɡ'nɪfɪkənt] unbedeutsam **expanse** [ɪk'spæns] Weite **grape** [ɡreɪp] Traube, Wein **arbor** ['ɑːbə] Laube **trellis** ['trelɪs] Spalier **occasionally** [ə'keɪʒnəlɪ] gelegentlich **amorphous** [ə'mɔːfəs] formlos **to cast** [kɑːst] werfen **beam** [biːm] Strahl **reflection** [rɪ'flekʃn] Spiegelung, Widerschein **delight** [dɪ'laɪt] Freude **to do honor to** ['ɒnə] j-m zur Ehre gereichen **derived from** [dɪ'raɪvd] abgeleitet von

"Blake!" he whispered. "Blake you were remembering. We read that months ago!"

Emma was silent. He heard her make a little bewildered sound in her **throat**, could feel all her being reaching **trustingly** toward him, helplessly toward him, thought he could see only the milky **glow** of her face in the dark.

He **was repulsed** by the thought that, overcome as she was now by the hypnosis of her words, she might come to him, her hands **groping** about his face. He could not have borne it... .

"But it was the voice I heard," she declared.

He had stood several seconds near motionless from the **anxiety** of the darkness. Now he began to regain **confidence**. "Since the child's **conception** was a miracle, it is fitting that his birth should be also," he remarked calmly, in the preacherlike tone he knew she loved. She bent forward as though drinking from a **spring**. His brain worked with clarity, with a **detachment** that shamed him. He remembered one evening when he had spoken of a crazy whirling picture in his brain which he was going to paint. It would be called *The Creation of the World*. Emma had followed him about the room, **savoring** the abstractness of his words, and he had retreated, babbling on and on and retreating until he was in a corner, and then he had told her to go back to her chair, and she had gone. And when he said to her, "Come here," she had come. He had sent her back and forth many times, until the game had frightened him and made him ashamed.

He reached his hand out to her. "Come," he said, "tell me about the miracle."

She came around the curve of the well. "Oh, he will be

---

throat [θrəʊt] Kehle **trustingly** ['trʌstɪŋlɪ] voller Vertrauen **glow** [gləʊ] Schimmern, Schein **to be repulsed** [rɪ'pʌlst] angewidert sein **to grope** [grəʊp] tastend suchen **anxiety** [əŋ'zaɪətɪ] Angst **confidence** ['kɒnfɪdəns] Zuversicht **conception** [kən'sepʃn] Empfängnis **spring** [sprɪŋ] Quelle **detachment** [dɪ'tætʃmənt] Gleichgültigkeit, Ungerührtheit **savoring** ['seɪvərɪŋ] genießend

brought forth only with the sweet pain of a **revelation**, spreading happiness beyond all measure."

"And if he were to appear in his time from the well, like a spirit emerging from the center of God's creation, then his coming would be miracle enough. He could command all the people who would wonder at his birth... . Isn't it so, Emma?"

"Yes!" She reached out for his hands. "*That* would be a miracle!"

"Yes." He did not realize how icy his hands were until he felt her warmth. "Destroy yourself, for your presence will make only confusion." He drew her nearer to the well **rim**, nearer to himself. "Otherwise the people's minds will be divided, for you are mortal... . Is it not a fitting thing the child should come forth of his own?"

There was a sharp crack from the road, as of a tree breaking.

He recoiled to the other side of the well. "What was that?" he whispered.

Emma had not taken her eyes from him. She leaned toward him, held to the well stones, and took a step toward him.

"Emma, don't look at me! What was that on the road?"

She turned her head in the direction he pointed, but she was not seeing, not listening for anything but the magic words.

The gate swung in the **soil**. Steps came slowly, grinding on the ground.

Arthur could hardly breathe. The miracle, the scales, the fantastic theater he had played in, were **dispelled**. He could not find himself. He was in **limbo**, and in his mind now was the paralyzing quiet. His brain was seized in the prison of his own evilness... . **Polluter**! destroyer! And no goodness ever! He drew his fingertips along the stones till he felt them bleed. The steps came closer—cautious, **flaring** eyes somewhere in the darkness.

---

revelation [ˌrevəˈleɪʃn] Enthüllung, Offenbarung **rim** [rɪm] Rand **soil** [sɔɪl] Boden, Erde **to dispel** [dɪˈspel] verscheuchen, auflösen **limbo** [ˈlɪmbəʊ] Vorhölle **polluter** [pəˈluːtə] Beschmutzer **flaring** [ˈflærɪŋ] flackernd

Emma heard the **crack** of his head in the **column** of the well, the **impact** of his body meeting the water. The air in the well shimmered like the water and settled into silence.

Dumbly Emma stood without stirring, dumb to the Negro's voice which said something to her as from an enormous distance. The **thread** that had guided her through the labyrinth of her world had been **severed**. She relaxed suddenly, broke into a wild scream that died like the **wail** of an animal lost in the woods.

She stumbled toward the house. "Oh, God!" she cried. "Look down on us! Oh, God, save us!"

---

crack [kræk] Bersten **column** ['kɒləm] Schacht **impact** ['ɪmpækt] Wucht **dumbly** ['dʌmlɪ] benommen **thread** [θred] (Leit-)Faden **to sever** ['sevə] durchtrennen **wail** [weɪl] Heulen, Wimmern

The Great Cardhouse

Lucien Montlehuc started a little when he saw the notice. He read it twice, slowly, and then, as if he finally believed it, put down his newspaper and removed his monocle. A **habitual** expression of amusement returned to his face, and his lids fluttered over his bright blue eyes. "Imagine Gaston Potin **taken in by** it!" he said to himself. "Of all people to be fooled!"

This thought made him even more **gleeful**. It would not be the first time that he had **proven** Gaston Potin **wrong**. This particular **Giotto** was a **forgery**, and Gaston was putting it up for sale as a **genuine**. Lucien meant to have it, and the sale was that very afternoon. How fortunate he had been to see the notice in time! The magnificent **counterfeit** might have slipped through his fingers again.

Lucien put his monocle back in the grip of his slightly **protruding** brow, **summoned** François and ordered him to pack their bags for an overnight stay in Aix-en-Provence. While he waited, he turned to *The **Revelation** to the **Shepherds*** in his book of Giotto reproductions and studied it. Again he thought how odd it was that poor Gaston Potin would not have suspected it to be a forgery. Perhaps it was the too-rigid faces of the kneeling shepherds that told him the painting was not from Giotto's hand. There was no real religious feeling there. The **annunciatory angel's** robe was a too-brilliant pink. The composition itself was not right, not Giotto—but it *was* magnificent, as a forgery. Lucien did not need a **magnifying glass**

---

habitual [hə'bɪtʃʊəl] gewohnheitsmäßig **to be taken in by s.th.** [ˌteɪkən‿'ɪn baɪ] auf etw. hereinfallen **gleeful** ['gli:fl] schadenfroh **to prove s.o. wrong** [pru:v … 'rɒŋ] j-n e-s Irrtums überführen **Giotto** ['dʒɔ:təʊ] *Ital. Maler und Bildhauer (1267–1337)* **forgery** ['fɔ:dʒərɪ] Fälschung **genuine** ['dʒenjʊɪn] Original **counterfeit** ['kaʊntəfɪt] Nachbildung **protruding** [prə'tru:dɪŋ] vorstehend **to summon** ['sʌmən] herbeirufen **revelation** [ˌrevə'leɪʃn] Erscheinung **shepherd** ['ʃepəd] Hirte **annunciatory angel** [ə'nʌnsɪətrɪ ˌeɪndʒl] Verkündigungsengel **magnifying glass** ['mægnɪfaɪɪŋ glɑ:s] Lupe

to **detect** a forgery. Something within him, some inner **sensory** apparatus, betrayed the **spurious** instantly and always. It never **failed**.

Besides, hadn't an Englishman, Sir Ronald Dunsenny, questioned the authenticity of this *Revelation* around the time of the Fruehlingen **purchase**? Indeed, Sir Ronald had **ventured** that the original had been destroyed in a fire in the middle of the eighteenth century! Evidently Gaston Potin didn't know that.

It was Lucien's passion to collect the most perfect imitations, and only the imitations, of the great artists. He did not want genuine paintings. And he **prided himself** that his **sham** masterpieces were such fine shams that any could, if presented as the original, fool the eyes of the most **astute** dealers and critics in the world.

Lucien had played many such tricks during the fifteen years he had been collecting forgeries. He might **submit** one of his forgeries as a **loan** from an individual who owned the original, for instance, then attend the exhibition and remark his **suspicions** publicly, to be proven right in the end, of course. Twice he had subjected Gaston Potin—with his great **reputation** as an art dealer—to such **embarrassment**. And once, Lucien had made Gaston uneasy about an original by presenting one of his forgeries that was so good it had taken six experts three days to decide which picture *was* the original. All in all, it had caused Gaston Potin to refer **scathingly** to Lucien's well-known collection and to his **lamentable** taste for the **bogus**. Lamentable to whom? Lucien wondered. And why? His **pranks** had cost him a few friendships, perhaps, but then he

---

to detect [dɪ'tekt] entdecken **sensory** ['sensərɪ] Sinnes- **spurious** ['spjʊərɪəs] unecht **to fail** [feɪl] fehlschlagen **purchase** ['pɜːtʃəs] Erwerbung, Kauf **to venture** ['ventʃə] (es) wagen (zu sagen) **to pride o.s.** [praɪd] stolz sein auf **sham** [ʃæm] Nachahmung **astute** [ə'stjuːt] scharfsinnig **to submit** [səb'mɪt] ausgeben als **loan** [ləʊn] Leihgabe **suspicion** [sə'spɪʃn] Verdacht **reputation** [ˌrepjʊ'teɪʃn] Ruf **embarrassment** [ɪm'bærəsmənt] Peinlichkeit **scathingly** ['skeɪðɪŋlɪ] vernichtend **lamentable** ['læməntəbl] bedauernswert **bogus** ['bəʊgəs] Schwindel **prank** [præŋk] Streich

cared as little for friendship as he cared for the true Leonardos, the true Renis, the true anything: friendship and **bona fide masterpieces** were too natural, too easy, too boring. Not that he actually disliked people, and people liked Lucien well enough, but if friendship threatened, Lucien **withdrew**.

His six-million-franc **Delahaye** sped along the Route Napoleon from Paris toward Aix at a hundred kilometers an hour. **Plane trees** in full leaf, their **smooth bark peeling** in purplish, pink, and beige **patches**, flickered by at the edges of the road like **picket fences**. A landscape of **dusky** orange and green and **tan**, the occasional blue of a farmer's cart—a landscape as beautifully composed as a Gobelin tapestry—unfolded continuously on right and left, but Lucien had no eye for it. Nature's creations did not interest him compared to man's, and his **stocky** body sat deep in the seat of the car. Today there was the Fruehlingen Giotto to think about, and he looked forward to the auction with the **keen**, **single-minded anticipation** of a hunter or a lover. **Merely** for Lucien Montlehuc to **bid** for a painting meant that the painting was, or most likely was, a counterfeit, and would in this case immediately throw suspicion upon Gaston, who was sponsoring the auction. Some of the **audience** at Aix might think he was trying to play another trick on Gaston, of course, by bidding. So much the better when the experts confirmed the falsity after the picture was his.

"Excellent **snails**," Lucien remarked with satisfaction, his pink cheeks glowing after his luncheon. He and François walked quickly to the car.

---

bona fide masterpiece [ˌbəʊnə faɪdɪ ˈmɑːstəpiːs] echtes Meisterwerk **to withdraw** [wɪðˈdrɔː] sich zurückziehen **Delahaye** [ˌdəlɑːˈheɪ] *Automarke* **plane tree** [ˈpleɪn triː] Platane **smooth** [smuːð] glatt **bark** [bɑːk] Rinde **to peel** [piːl] (sich) schälen **patch** [pætʃ] Flecken **picket fence** [ˈpɪkɪt fens] Lattenzaun **dusky** [ˈdʌskɪ] dunkel **tan** [tæn] gelbbraun **stocky** [ˈstɒkɪ] stämmig **keen** [kiːn] eifrig, bestrebt **single-minded** [ˌsɪŋglˈmaɪndɪd] zielstrebig **anticipation** [ænˌtɪsɪˈpeɪʃn] Vorfreude **merely** [ˈmɪəlɪ] allein schon **to bid** [bɪd] setzen auf, (i. e-r Auktion) bieten **audience** [ˈɔːdɪəns] Publikum **snail** [sneɪl] Schnecke

"Excellent, monsieur," François replied agreeably. His good humor reflected that of his master. François was tall and **lean** and **congenitally** lazy, though he never failed to carry out an order from Lucien. He had not forgotten that he **had** once **been earmarked** for execution by the Spanish government for being in possession of a false passport. Because François had been amused and cool about the whole thing, he had won Lucien's **admiration**, and Lucien had managed to buy his freedom. Since then François, actually a Russian who had escaped to Czechoslovakia with a price on his head, had lived in France, safe and **content** to be alive and in Lucien's employ.

Lucien himself had once lived in Czechoslovakia. In 1926, most European papers had carried an **account** of a very young Captain Lucas Minchovik, a **soldier of fortune** who had been **severely wounded** in a **skirmish** on the Yugoslav border. Years ago, in Czechoslovakia, people had sometimes asked him about the 1926 report, the young captain's heroism having made the story **memorable**, but Lucien had always **disclaimed** any knowledge of it. It had been another soldier of the same name, he said. Finally, he had changed his name and come to France.

In Aix, Lucien and François stopped first at the Hôtel des Étrangers to reserve a three-room suite, then drove on to the Musée de Tapisserie beside the Cathedral Saint-Sauveur. The auction was to be held in the open court of the *musée,* and was **scheduled** to begin in half an hour, but things in Aix were always late. Cars of all sizes and **manufacture cluttered** the narrow streets around the cathedral, and the courtyard

---

lean [liːn] schlank **congenitally** [kən'dʒenɪtlɪ] von Geburt (an) **to be earmarked** ['ɪəmɑːkt] bestimmt, vorgesehen sein für **admiration** [ˌædmə'reɪʃn] Bewunderung **content** [kən'tent] zufrieden **account** [ə'kaʊnt] Bericht **soldier of fortune** [ˌsəʊldʒə əv 'fɔːtʃən] Söldner **severely wounded** [sɪˌvɪəlɪ 'wuːndɪd] schwer verletzt **skirmish** ['skɜːmɪʃ] Geplänkel, Scharmützel **memorable** ['memərəbl] denkwürdig, unvergesslich **to disclaim** [dɪs'kleɪm] leugnen **scheduled** ['ʃedjuːld] (im Zeitplan) vorgesehen, eingeplant **manufacture** [ˌmænʊ'fæktʃə] (Auto-)Marke **to clutter** ['klʌtə] verstopfen

was a **bedlam** of hurrying workmen and **chattering** agents and **dealers** and private buyers who had not yet begun to seat themselves.

"Do you see M. Potin?" Lucien asked François, who was a good deal taller than Lucien.

"No, monsieur."

An **acquaintance** of Lucien's, a dealer from Strasbourg, told him that M. Potin was giving a luncheon at his villa just outside the town, and that he had not yet arrived.

Lucien decided to pay Gaston Potin a visit. He was eager to let Gaston know of his interest in the Giotto. As they drew up to Gaston's Villa Madeleine, Lucien heard the **treble** notes of a piano from within. **Faint** but **bell-like**, it was a Scarlatti sonata. He was shown into the hall by a servant. Through the open door of the salon, Lucien saw a **slender** woman seated at the piano, and **a score of** men and a few women standing or sitting motionless, listening to her. Lucien paused at the **threshold**, adjusted his monocle, and **espied** Gaston just behind the piano, concentrating on the music with an expression of **rapt** and sentimental enjoyment. Lucien's eyes swept the rest of the company. They were all here—Font-Martigue of the Dauberville Gallery in Paris, Fritz Heber of Vienna, Martin Palmer of London. Certainly the **cream**.

And they were all listening to the sonata—with the same **absorption** as Gaston. Lucien's appearance in the doorway had not even been noticed. The fast movement the woman was playing was splendid indeed. The notes **sparkled** from her fingers like drops of pure springwater. But to Lucien's ear,

---

bedlam ['bedləm] Chaos, Tumult **to chatter** ['tʃætə] plaudern **dealer** ['di:lə] Händler **acquaintance** [ə'kweɪntəns] Bekannter **treble** ['trebl] Diskant, Sopran **faint** [feɪnt] schwach **bell-like** ['bellaɪk] glockengleich **slender** ['slendə] schlank **a score of** [skɔ:] e-e große Zahl von **threshold** ['θreʃhəʊld] Schwelle **to espy** [e'spaɪ] erspähen **rapt** [ræpt] versunken, hingerissen **cream** [kri:m] *hier:* die 'Crème de la crème', gehobene Gesellschaft **absorption** [əb'sɔ:pʃn] Hingabe, Versunkenheit **to sparkle** ['spɑ:kl] perlen

which was as **infallible** as his eye, an **ingredient** was missing—a pleasure in the **performance**. It was **audible** to Lucien that she **detested** Scarlatti, if not music itself. Lucien smiled. Could she really be holding the company as **spellbound** as it looked? But of course she was. How **obtuse** people were, even those who professed a knowledge of the arts! There was a perfect crash of applause from the little audience when she finished.

Lucien saw Gaston coming toward him with the pianist on his arm. Gaston smiled at Lucien as if the music had made him forget that there had ever been unpleasantnesses between them.

"Very happy and surprised to see you, Lucien!" Gaston said. "May I present the music teacher of my childhood—Mlle. Claire Duhamel of Aix."

"Enchanté, mademoiselle," said Lucien. He observed with satisfaction the stir of interest his entry into the salon had caused.

"She plays superbly, doesn't she?" Gaston went on. "She has just been asked to give a series of concerts in Paris, but she has refused, *n'est-ce pas*, Mlle. Claire? Aix should not **be deprived of** your music for so long!"

Lucien smiled politely, then said, "I learned of your sale only this morning, Gaston. Why didn't you send me an **announcement**?"

"Because I was sure there is nothing here that would interest you. These are all authentic pictures of my own choosing."

"But *The Revelation to the Shepherds* interests me *enor-*

---

infallible [ɪn'fæləbl] untrügerisch, unfehlbar **ingredient** [ɪn'griːdɪənt] Bestandteil, Zutat **performance** [pə'fɔːməns] Darbietung **audible** ['ɔːdəbl] hörbar **to detest** [dɪ'test] verabscheuen **spellbound** ['spelbaʊnd] verzaubert **obtuse** [əb'tjuːs] stumpf **to be deprived of s.th.** [dɪ'praɪvd] e-r Sache entbehren **announcement** [ə'naʊnsmənt] Ankündigung

mously!" Lucien told him with a smile. "I don't suppose if it's here you might let me see it now."

Behind Gaston's **frank** surprise, there was just the **least** alarm. "But with the greatest pleasure, Lucien. Follow me."

Mlle. Duhamel, who had been gazing at Lucien all the while, checked him with the question, "Are you an admirer of Giotto, too, M. Montlehuc?"

Lucien looked at her. She was a typical *vieille femme*—an old maid—of a Provençal town, **drab** and shy, yet with an air of **tenacious purpose** in her own narrow, **cramped** way of life, a look of **wiry vigor** that suggested a plant growing at the edge of a **wind-whipped** cliff. Gentle, sad gray eyes looked out of her small face with such depression of spirit that one wanted to turn away immediately, because of an inability to help her. A less attractive person Lucien could not have imagined. "Yes, mademoiselle," he said, and hurried after Gaston.

Lucien's first sight of the picture brought that **leap** of excitement and **recognition** that only the finest forgeries gave him. From the patina, he judged the picture to be more than two hundred years old. And today it would be his.

"You see?" Gaston smiled **confidently**.

Lucien sighed, in **mock defeat**. "I see. A beautiful piece indeed. My congratulations, Gaston."

Lucien attended the auction in the **subdued** manner of one who watches from the outside, a bystander. He waited with impatience while an **indifferent Messina** and a miserable "Ignoto Veneziano" from the Fruehlingen collection were put up and

---

frank [fræŋk] ehrlich **least** *sup. von* **little** [liːst, 'lɪtl] *hier:* e-e Spur von **drab** [dræb] grau, farblos **tenacious** [tə'neɪʃəs] zäh, hartnäckig **purpose** ['pɜːpəs] Ziel, Zweck **cramped** ['kræmpt] verkrampft **wiry** ['waɪərɪ] drahtig **vigor** ['vɪgə] Kraft, Energie **wind-whipped** ['wɪndwɪpd] windgepeitscht **leap** [liːp] Freudensprung **recognition** [ˌrekəg'nɪʃn] Wiedererkennen **confidently** ['kɒnfɪdəntlɪ] vertrauensselig **in mock defeat** [mɒk dɪ'fiːt] scheinbar besiegt **subdued** [səb'djuːd] unterwürfig, gedämpft **indifferent** [ɪn'dɪfrənt] unbedeutend **Messina (Antonello da ...)** [mes'siːnə (ˌɑːntɔː'nellɔː da)] *Ital. Maler der Renaissance, 1430–1490*

sold. Apart from the false Giotto, Lucien thought **mischievously**, the Barons von Fruehlingen did have **execrable** taste!

Mlle. Duhamel, on a **bench** against the side wall, was again staring at him, he noticed, with what thoughts behind her quiet gray eyes, he could not guess. Lucien found something **disturbing**, something arrogantly **omniscient** in her **scrutiny**. For an instant, he **resented** her **fiercely** and **unreasonably**. Lucien removed his monocle and passed his fingertips lightly across his lids. When he looked up again, the *Revelation* was on the **dais**.

A man whom Lucien could not see bid a million new francs.

"A million and a half," said Lucien calmly. He was in the last row.

Heads turned to look at him. There was a murmur as the crowd recognized Lucien Montlehuc.

"Two million!" cried the same unseen bidder.

"Two million ten thousand," replied Lucien, intending to provoke laughter, as he did, by the **insultingly** small **raise**. He heard the **sibilant** whisper of "Lucien" among the crowd. Someone laughed, a **sardonic** laugh that made a corner of Lucien's mouth go up in response. Lucien knew from the rising hum that people had begun to ask one another if the Giotto were **indisputably** genuine.

The unseen bidder stood up. It was Font-Martigue of Paris. His bald head turned its **eagle** profile for a moment to glance at Lucien coldly. "Three million."

Lucien also stood up. "Three million five hundred."

"Three million seven," replied Font-Martigue, more to Lucien than to the auctioneer.

---

mischievously ['mɪstʃɪvəslɪ] boshaft **execrable** ['eksɪkrəbl] abscheulich **bench** [bentʃ] Bank **disturbing** [dɪ'stɜːbɪŋ] beunruhigend **omniscient** [ɒm'nɪsɪənt] allwissend **scrutiny** ['skruːtɪnɪ] genaue Beobachtung **to resent s.o.** [rɪ'zent] j-n abstoßend finden **fiercely** ['fɪəslɪ] heftig **unreasonably** [ʌn'riːznəblɪ] unvernünftig **dais** ['deɪɪs] Podium **insultingly** [ɪn'sʌltɪŋlɪ] unverschämt **raise** [reɪz] Anstieg, Erhöhung (d-s Gebots) **sibilant** ['sɪbɪlənt] zischend **sardonic** [sɑː'dɒnɪk] hämisch **indisputably** [ˌɪndɪ'spjuːtəblɪ] unbestreitbar **eagle** ['iːgl] Adler

Lucien raised it to three million eight hundred and Font-Martigue to four million.

"And a hundred thousand," added Lucien.

At this rate, the figure might be driven beyond the price of a genuine Giotto, but Lucien did not care. The joke on Gaston would be worth it. And the audience **was wavering** already. Only Font-Martigue was bidding. Everyone knew that Gaston Potin had been wrong a few times, but Lucien never.

"Four million two hundred thousand," said Font-Martigue.

"Four million three," said Lucien.

The audience **tittered**. Lucien wished he could see Gaston at this moment, but he couldn't. Gaston was doubtless in the front row with his back to Lucien. A pity. It was no longer a **contest** of bidding. It had become a **contest** of faith versus nonfaith, of believer versus nonbeliever. Fifteen meters away on the dais the *Revelation* stood like a **reliquary** in its **golden-leaf** frame, a reliquary of the divine fire of art—as each of them saw it.

"Four million four," said Font-Martigue in a tone of **finality**.

"Four million five," Lucien promptly replied.

Font-Martigue folded his arms and sat down.

The auctioneer **rapped**. "Four million five hundred thousand new francs?"

Lucien smiled. Who could afford to outbid him when he wanted something?

"Four million six," said a voice on Lucien's left.

A man who looked like a young Charles de Gaulle leaned forward on his knees, **focusing** his attention on the auctioneer. Lucien knew the type, the de Gaulle type indeed, another believer, an idealist. He was in for five million francs at least.

Five minutes later, the auctioneer pronounced *The Revela-*

---

to be wavering ['weɪvərɪŋ] unschlüssig sein **to titter** ['tɪtə] kichern **contest** ['kɒntest] Wettstreit **reliquary** ['relɪkwərɪ] Reliquie **golden-leaf** [ˌgəʊldn'liːf] Blattgold **finality** [faɪ'nælətɪ] Bestimmtheit **to rap** [ræp] klopfen, mit d. Hammer schlagen **to focus** ['fəʊkəs] zentrieren

tion to the Shepherds the **property** of Lucien Montlehuc for the sum of five million two hundred and fifty thousand new francs.

Lucien came forward immediately to write his check and to take possession.

"My congratulations, Lucien," Gaston Potin said. His forehead was **damp** with **perspiration**, but he managed a bewildered smile. "A genuine work of art at last. The only one in your collection, I'm sure."

"What is genuine?" Lucien asked. "Is art genuine? What is more **sincere** than imitation, Gaston?"

"Do you mean to say you think this painting is a forgery?"

"If it is not, I shall give it back to you. What would I want with it if it were genuine? You know, though, you should not have represented it as a genuine painting. It ran my price up."

Gaston's face was growing pink. "There are a dozen men here who could prove you wrong, Lucien."

"I invite them to prove me wrong," Lucien said **courteously**. "Seriously, Gaston, ask them to come to my suite at the Hôtel des Étrangers for aperitifs this afternoon. Let them bring their magnifying glasses and their history books. At six o'-clock: May I expect you?"

"You *may,*" said Gaston Potin.

Lucien walked out of the courtyard to his waiting car. François had already strapped the *Revelation* carefully between the seat back and the spare tire. Lucien happened to look behind him as he reached the car. He saw Mlle. Duhamel walking slowly from the doorway of the courtyard toward him, and he felt a **throb** in his chest, a strange **premonition**. Sunlight, broken into **droplets** by the trees, played like silent music over her moving figure, light and quick as her own fin-

---

property ['prɒpətɪ] Eigentum **damp** [dæmp] feucht **perspiration** [ˌpɜːspə'reɪʃn] Schweiß **sincere** [sɪn'sɪə] aufrichtig **courteously** ['kɜːtjəslɪ] höflich **throb** [θrɒb] Pochen **premonition** [ˌpriːmə'nɪʃn] Vorahnung **droplet** ['drɒplət] Tröpfchen

gers had played in Gaston's salon. He remembered his feeling, as he listened to her Scarlatti sonata, that she **loathed** playing it. And yet to play so brilliantly! That took a kind of genius, Lucien thought. He was aware suddenly of a great respect for Mlle. Duhamel, and of something else, something he could not identify, perhaps **compassion**. It pained him that anyone with Mlle. Duhamel's ability should take so little joy in it, that she should look so **crushed**, so **agonizingly self-effacing**.

"Do you know that I am receiving some friends at six o'clock this afternoon, Mlle. Duhamel?" Lucien said with an **unwonted awkwardness** as she came closer. "I should be honored if you would join us."

Mlle. Duhamel accepted with pleasure.

"Come a little early, if you will."

"Five million two hundred and fifty thousand francs for a counterfeit," Mlle. Duhamel whispered with **awe**. She sat on the edge of a chair in the salon of Lucien's suite, **gazing at** the picture Lucien had leaned against the divan.

Lucien strolled back and forth before her, smiling, smoking a Turkish cigarette. François had gone out a few moments before to fetch Cinzano and pâté and biscuits, and now they were alone. Mlle. Duhamel had been surprised, but not overly surprised, when he told her the Giotto was a forgery. Her reaction had been exactly right. And now she regarded the picture with the respect that was **due** it.

"One usually pays more dearly for the false than for the true, mademoiselle," Lucien said, feeling **expansive** in his hour of triumph. "This hair I touch, for instance," he said, patting the top of his light brown, gently waving hair, "is a

---

to loathe [ləʊð] verabscheuen **compassion** [kəm'pæʃn] Mitgefühl **crushed** ['krʌʃt] niedergeschlagen **agonizingly** ['ægənaɪzɪŋlɪ] qualvoll **self-effacing** [ˌselfɪ'feɪsɪŋ] zurückhaltend **unwonted** [ʌn'wəʊntɪd] ungewöhnlich **awkwardness** ['ɔːkwədnəs] Unbeholfenheit **awe** [ɔː] Ehrfurcht **to gaze at** [geɪz] blicken auf **due** [djuː] angemessen, gebührend **expansive** [ɪk'spænsɪv] mitteilsam

toupee, the finest that Paris can make. Grown by nature, it would have cost nothing. Strictly speaking, it would have been worthless. It *is* worthless, to a man with hair of his own. But when I must buy it to hide a **deficiency** of nature, I must pay a hundred and fifty thousand francs for it. And it is a just price, when one thinks of the **skill** and **labor** that went into its creation." Lucien swept off his toupee and held it in his hand, **lustrous** side uppermost. His **bald crown** was a healthy pink-tan, like his face, and really detracted little from the liveliness of his appearance, which was extraordinary for his age. The bald head was a surprise, that was all.

"I had no idea you wore a toupee, M. Montlehuc."

Lucien eyed her sharply. He thought he saw amusement in her **tilted** head. She had one element of charm, he **conceded**: she had humor. "And applying this same principle to the false Giotto," Lucien continued, inspired by Mlle. Duhamel's attention, "we might say Giotto's genius was a thing of nature, too, a gift of the gods, perhaps, but certainly a faculty which cost him nothing, and in a sense cost him no effort, since he created as every artist creates, out of necessity. But consider the poor mortal who created this almost perfect imitation. Think of his **travail** in reproducing every stroke of the master exactly! Consider *his* effort!"

Mlle. Duhamel was absorbing every word. "Yes," she said.

"You understand then why I **value** the imitators so highly, or rather give them their proper value?"

"I understand," she answered.

Lucien felt perhaps she did. "And you, Mlle. Duhamel, may I say that is why I find you so valuable? You have a superb talent for **deceiving**. Your performance of Scarlatti this after-

---

deficiency [dɪ'fɪʃnsɪ] Unzulänglichkeit **skill** [skɪl] Geschicklichkeit **labor** ['leɪbə] Mühe **lustrous** ['lʌstrəs] glänzend **bald** [bɔːld] kahl **crown** [kraʊn] Schädel **tilted** ['tɪltɪd] zur Seite geneigt **to concede** [kən'siːd] einräumen **travail** *(Frz.)* ['træveɪl] Mühe **to value** ['væljuː] wertschätzen **to deceive** [dɪ'siːv] täuschen

noon was by no means inferior to the best—technically. It was inferior in only one respect." He hesitated, wondering if he dared go on.

"Yes?" Mlle. Duhamel **prompted**, a little fearfully.

"You hated it, didn't you?"

She looked down at her slim, **tense** hands in her **lap**, hands that were still as smooth and flexible as a young girl's. "Yes. Yes, I hated it. I hate music. It's—" She stopped. Her eyes had grown shiny with tears, but she held her head up and the tears did not drop.

Lucien smiled nervously. He was not good at **comforting** people, but he wanted to comfort Mlle. Duhamel and did not know how to begin. "What a silly thing to cry about!" he burst out. "Such a talent! You play exquisitely! Why, if you could endure the boredom— and I really admire you for not being able to endure it—you might play in concerts all over the world! I daresay not a music critic in a thousand would recognize your real feelings. And what would he do if he did? Make some **trifling** comment that's all. But your playing would **enchant** millions and millions of people. Just as my forgeries could enchant millions and millions of people." He laughed and, before he realized what he did, put out his hand and pressed her thin shoulder **affectionately**.

She shuddered under his touch and relaxed in her chair. She seemed to shrink until she was nothing but that small, unhappy **core** of herself. "You are the only one who has ever known," she said. "It was my father who made me study music as a child and as a young girl, study and study until I had no time to do anything else—even to make a friend. My father was organist of the church here in Aix. He wanted me to be a concert pianist, but I knew I never could be, because I hated

---

to prompt [prɒmpt] unverzüglich antworten **tense** [tens] angespannt **lap** [læp] Schoß **to comfort** ['kʌmfət] trösten **trifling** ['traɪflɪŋ] oberflächlich, belanglos **to enchant** [ɪn'tʃɑːnt] bezaubern **affectionately** [ə'fekʃnətlɪ] liebevoll **core** [kɔː] Innerste,s

music too much. And finally—I was thirty-eight when my father died—it was too late to think of marriage. So I stayed on in the village, earning my living in the only way I could, by teaching music. And how ashamed I am! To pretend to love what I hate! To teach others to love what I hate—the piano!"

Her voice trailed off on "piano" like a **plaintive sob** itself.

"You fooled Gaston," Lucien reminded her, smiling. An excitement, a joy of life was rising in him. He could not stand still. He wanted—he did not know exactly what he wanted to do, except to **convince** Mlle. Duhamel that she was wrong to feel ashamed, wrong to torture herself inwardly. "Don't you see it isn't at all logical," he began, "to take seriously something you were never serious about in the first place?—Look, mademoiselle!" With a **graceful** movement, Lucien removed his right hand. He held the **detached** and perfectly natural-looking right hand in his left. His right arm ended in an empty white **cuff**.

Mlle. Duhamel **gasped**.

"You never suspected that, did you?" asked Lucien, grinning like a schoolboy who has brought off a practical joke with success.

"No." Obviously, Mlle. Duhamel hadn't suspected that.

"You see, it's exactly the **mate** of the left, and by certain movements which have now become automatic, I can give the impression that my useless hand cooperates with the other." Lucien replaced his hand quickly.

"Why, it's like a miracle!" Mlle. Duhamel said.

"A miracle of modern plastics, that's all. And my right foot, I might add, too." Lucien pulled up his trouser leg a few inches, though there was nothing to be seen but a normal-looking black shoe and sock. "I was wounded once, **literally** blown apart, but should I have **crept** about the world like a

---

plaintive ['pleɪntɪv] klagend **sob** [sɒb] Seufzer **to convince** [kən'vɪns] überzeugen **graceful** ['greɪsfl] anmutig **detached** [dɪ'tætʃt] losgelöst **cuff** [kʌf] Manschette **to gasp** [gɑːsp] staunen **mate** [meɪt] Gegenstück **literally** ['lɪtrəlɪ] buchstäblich **crept** *Pret.* **to creep** [krept, kriːp] kriechen

crab, **disgusting** everyone, an object of horror and pity? Life is to be enjoyed, is it not? Life is to give and take pleasure, is it not? You give pleasure, Mlle. Duhamel. It remains only for you to take it!" Lucien gave a great laugh that was so truly out of his heart, that rolled so solidly from his broad chest, Mlle. Duhamel began to smile, too.

Then she laughed. At first, her laugh was no more than a feeble **crack**, like the opening of a door that had been closed for an **incalculable** length of time. But the laugh grew, seemed to reach out in all directions, like a separate being taking form, taking courage.

"And my ear!" Lucien went on with delight. "It wasn't necessary to have two ears to hear what I heard in your music, mademoiselle. An excellent **match**, is it not, of my left ear? But not too perfect, because ears are never exactly alike." He could not remove his **grafted** right ear, but he **pinched** it and **winked at** her. "And my right eye—I will **spare** you that, but **suffice it** to say that it's made of glass. People often speak of my 'magic monocle' when they mention my **uncanny** judgments. I wear the monocle as a joke, by way of adding an **insult to an injury**, as the English would say. Can you tell the difference between my eyes, Mlle. Duhamel?" Lucien bent forward and looked into her gray eyes that were beginning to glow behind the tears.

"Indeed, I cannot," she told him.

Lucien beamed with satisfaction. "Did I say my foot? My entire *leg* is of **hollow** plastic!" Lucien struck his **thigh** with a pencil he picked up from the table, and it gave a hollow **report**. "But does it stop me from dancing? And did anyone ever

---

crab [kræb] Krebs **to disgust** [dɪs'gʌst] abstoßen **crack** [kræk] Überschlagen (d. Stimme) **incalculable** [ɪn'kælkjʊləbl] unermesslich **match** [mætʃ] Gegenstück **grafted** ['grɑːftɪd] transplantiert **to pinch** [pɪntʃ] zwicken **to wink at s.o.** [wɪŋk] j-m zuzwinkern **to spare** [speə] (ver-)schonen **suffice it** [sə'faɪs] es möge genügen **uncanny** [ʌn'kænɪ] unheimlich **to add insult to injury** [ˌæd 'ɪnsʌlt tə 'ɪndʒərɪ] zusätzlich zu allem Übel, *hier:* um noch eins draufzusetzen **hollow** ['hɒləʊ] hohl **thigh** [θaɪ] Oberschenkel **report** [rɪ'pɔːt] *hier:* Widerhall

suggest that I **limp**? I don't limp. Shall I go on?" His **affirmative** clap of laughter came again.

Mlle. Duhamel looked at him, fascinated. "I've never—"

"Needless to say, my teeth!" Lucien interrupted her. "I had scarcely three whole teeth left after my injury. I was a young man then. But that doesn't matter, I saved my employer's life, and he **rewarded** me with a **trust fund** that enables me to spend my life in luxury. Anyway, my teeth are the product of an artist in deception, a Japanese whose **ingenuity** and powers of **depiction** certainly rank him with the great Leonardo. His name is Tao Mishugawa, but few on earth will ever hear of him. My teeth are full of faults, of course, like real ones. Every so often, just to deceive myself, I go to Tao and have some more fillings or an inlay put in. Tell me, mademoiselle, did you suspect?"

"I certainly did not," she assured him sincerely.

"If I could remove every artificial part of myself including the silver shin of my other leg and my plastic ribs, there wouldn't be much left of me, would there? Except the spirit. There would be *that* even more than now, I think! Does it seem strange to you that I speak of the spirit, Mlle. Duhamel?"

"Not at all. Of course it doesn't."

"I knew it wouldn't. There was no need to ask. You, too, are among the great in spirit, who respond to **challenge** and make nature appear **niggardly**. Your hours of tortured practice at the piano are not lost, mademoiselle. Not because of these words I say to you, but because you gave pleasure to a score of people this afternoon. Because you are able to give pleasure!"

---

to limp [lɪmp] hinken **affirmative** [əˈfɜːmətɪv] bestätigend, positiv **to reward s.o.** [rɪˈwɔːd] j-n belohnen **trust fund** [ˈtrʌst fʌnd] Treuhandvermögen **ingenuity** [ˌɪndʒəˈnjuːətɪ] Genialität **depiction** [dɪˈpɪkʃn] bildliche Darstellung **challenge** [ˈtʃælɪndʒ] Herausforderung **niggardly** [ˈnɪgədlɪ] armselig, kümmerlich

Mlle. Duhamel looked down at her hands again, but now there was a flush of her own pleasure in her cheeks.

"The critics and the art dealers call me a dilettante, the idiots! That I am an artist escapes them, of course. Let it! They are the real dilettanti, the do-nothings. You understand me because you are like me, Mlle. Duhamel, but all those who **sneer**, who stare, who laugh at me and **envy** and admire me at once because I am not ashamed to confess what I love— And here they are now!"

Someone had rapped on the door.

Lucien glanced at his watch. François was having trouble finding the right kind of pâté, perhaps. Lucien did not like to answer his door himself.

Mlle. Duhamel stood up. "May I open the door for your guests?"

Lucien stared at her. She looked taller than before, and almost—he could hardly believe it—happy. The glow he had seen in her gray eyes seemed to have spread through her entire body. Lucien, too, felt a happiness he had never known before. Perhaps the kind of happiness an artist feels after creating something, he thought, an artist whose talent is given by nature.

"I should be honored," Lucien said.

Gaston had come, and with him four other dealers, one of whom carried a picture which Lucien recognized as Giotto's ***Magi** in Bethlehem* from a private collection. Lucien greeted them **hospitably**. Then more people arrived, and finally François with the refreshments. The man with the picture set it next to Lucien's against the divan, and all got out their magnifying glasses.

"I assure you, you possess an original," Gaston said cheer-

---

to sneer [snɪə] höhnen **to envy** ['envɪ] beneiden **Magi** *Pl. von* **Magus** *(Lat.)* ['meɪdʒaɪ] 'Die 3 Weisen aus dem Morgenland' **hospitably** [hɒ'spɪtəblɪ] gastfreundlich

fully to Lucien. "Not that you didn't pay a fitting price for it." All of Gaston's confidence had returned.

Lucien gestured with his false hand at the group beside the divan. "The experts have not said so yet, have they? Let their magnifying glasses discover what I can see with my naked eyes." He strolled off toward Mlle. Duhamel and M. Palissy, who were talking in a corner of the room. How charming she looked, Lucien thought. A half hour ago, she would have been afraid to use her beautiful hands to **gesture** as she spoke.

Gaston **intercepted** Lucien before he reached Mlle. Duhamel. "You agree that this picture is genuine, Lucien?" he said, pointing to the picture the dealer had brought.

"Certainly," said Lucien, "That *Magi*—a careless piece of work, I've always thought, but certainly genuine."

"Examine the **brushstrokes**, Lucien. Compare them with the brushstrokes on your picture. It's so obvious, a child could see it. There is a fault in the brush that he used to paint the backgrounds of both pictures, a couple of **bristles** that made a **scratch** here and there. Evidently these pictures were painted at about the same time. It's the general opinion that they were, you know." Gaston stooped down beside the pictures. "One doesn't even need a magnifying glass to see it. But I had some photographs made and enlarged, just to be sure. Here they are, Lucien."

Lucien ignored the photographs on the divan. He could see it, with his good eye; a hair-line scratch here and there with an even finer scratch beside it, the scratches of a single brushstroke, made by the same brush. It was the same in both pictures, like a **pattern**, **obvious** enough when one looked for it, yet not obvious enough to be worthy of forging. Lucien's head grew **swimmy**. For an instant, he felt only a keen

---

to gesture ['dʒestʃə] gestikulieren **to intercept** [ˌɪntə'sept] abfangen **brushstroke** ['brʌʃstrəʊk] Pinselstrich, -führung **bristle** ['brɪsl] Borste, Pinselhaar **scratch** [skrætʃ] Kratzer **pattern** ['pætn] Muster **obvious** ['ɒbvɪəs] offensichtlich **swimmy** ['ʃwɪmɪ] leicht benommen

discomfort. He was aware that the eyes of everyone in the room were upon him as he bent over the two pictures. Most painfully of all, he was aware of Mlle. Duhamel. He felt he had failed her. He had been proven **fallible**.

"Now you see," said Gaston calmly, without **malice**, merely as if he were pointing out something that Lucien might have seen from the first.

Lucien felt as if a house of cards were **tumbling down** inside him, all that was himself, in fact. He could see now, looking at the picture he had believed to be false, that a **misconception**—a quick, initial misconception—was possible. Just as it would have been equally possible to judge the picture correctly, as he did now, and to sense that it was genuine. But he had made the misjudgment.

Lucien turned to the room. "I admit my error," he said, his tongue as dry as ashes.

He had expected laughter, but there was only a murmur, a kind of sigh in the room. He would rather they had laughed at him. No, at least there was one exchange of smiles, one nod of satisfaction from Font-Martigue that Lucien Montlehuc could be wrong. Lucien would have felt quite lost if he had not seen it. Yet no one seemed to realize the catastrophe that was taking place inside him. The great cardhouse was still falling. For the first time in his life, he felt near tears. He had a vision of himself without his **artifices**, without his arrogant faith in his infallibility—a piece of a man, unable even to stand upright, a miserable fragment. For a few moments, Lucien's spirit bore the full weight of reality, and almost broke beneath it.

"If you'd like to sell it back, of course, Lucien," Gaston's voice said kindly, distantly, whispering into the false ear, "I'll pay you the same price—"

---

discomfort [dɪs'kʌmfət] Unbehagen **fallible** ['fæləbl] fehlbar **malice** ['mælɪs] Böswilligkeit **to tumble down** [ˌtʌmbl 'daʊn] zusammenbrechen, einstürzen **misconception** [ˌmɪskən'sepʃn] Missverständnis, Fehleinschätzung **artifice** ['ɑːtɪfɪs] Kunstgriff, Künstlichkeit

"No. No, thank you, Gaston." Now he was being unreasonable **to boot**! What did he want with a genuine painting? Lucien **stumbled** toward Mlle. Duhamel. He stumbled on his artificial leg.

Mlle. Duhamel's face was as calm as if nothing had happened. "Why don't you tell them you were **pretending**?" she asked him, out of hearing of the others. "Why don't you pretend the whole afternoon was a great joke?"

Her face was even victorious, Lucien thought. He looked at it for a long moment, trying to draw strength from it, and failing. "But I wasn't joking," he said.

Then the guests were gone. Only he and Mlle. Duhamel remained. And the genuine Giotto. François, who had witnessed his master's **defeat**, standing in the background like a silent tragic chorus, had excused himself last of all and gone out.

Lucien sat down heavily on the divan.

"I shall keep the painting," Lucien said slowly, and with quiet, profound bitterness. He did not recognize his own voice, though he recognized that it was his real voice. It was the voice of the fragment of a man. "It will be the one original that will **spoil** the **purity** of my forgeries. Nothing in life is pure. Nothing is one thing and nothing more. Nothing is absolute. When I was a young man, I believed no bullet would ever touch me. And then one day I was struck by a grenade. I thought I could never misjudge a painting. And today a public misjudgment!"

"But didn't you know that nothing is absolute? Why, even my **kitten** knows that much!"

Lucien glanced at Mlle. Duhamel with the **fiercest impatience**. He had scarcely been aware of her the past few moments. Now he **resented** her presence as much as he had when she had spoken to him first in Gaston's salon.

---

to boot *obs.* [buːt] noch dazu, obendrein **to stumble** ['stʌmbl] stolpern **to pretend** [prɪ'tend] vortäuschen **defeat** [dɪ'fiːt] Niederlage **to spoil** [spɔɪl] verderben **purity** ['pjʊərətɪ] Reinheit **kitten** ['kɪtn] junges Kätzchen **fierce** [fɪəs] scharf, heftig **impatience** [ɪm'peɪʃns] Ungeduld **to resent s.th.** [rɪ'zent] etw. unangenehm finden

She was standing by the little three-legged console table where lay her green string **gloves** and her big square pocketbook that was as flat as her own body. She looked at him anxiously, as if she were puzzled for a moment as to what to do. Then she came toward him, sat down beside him on the divan, and took his hand in hers. It happened to be his false hand, but she **betrayed** no surprise, if she felt any. She held his hand affectionately, as if it were real.

Lucien started to take his hand away, but only sighed instead. What did it matter? But then, with the touch he could not feel, he realized another misjudgment, a much older one. He had thought he could never feel close to any human being, never allow himself to be close. But now he did feel close to Mlle. Duhamel. He felt closer to her than François, the only other person who knew of the great cardhouse that was Lucien Montlehuc. François had not suffered as Mlle. Duhamel had suffered, the idiot. It was a **tenderness** he felt for Mlle. Duhamel, and admiration. She lived within a cardhouse, too. Yet, if nothing was absolute, a cardhouse was not absolute, either. He might rebuild it, but it would never be perfect, and had never been perfect. How stupid he had been! He who had always prided himself that he knew the imperfections of everything, even art. Lucien looked down in wonder at his and Mlle. Duhamel's **clasped** hands. It had been so many years since he had had a friend.

His heart began to **thump** like a lover's. How pleasant it would be, Lucien thought suddenly, to have Mlle. Duhamel in his home, to have her play for him and his guests, to give her luxuries that she had never been able to afford. Lucien smiled, for the thought had only flitted across his mind like the shadow of a bird across the grass. Marriage, indeed! Hadn't he just realized that nothing was ever perfect? Why should he try to better what couldn't be bettered—the happiness he felt with Mlle. Duhamel at this instant?

---

glove [glʌv] Handschuh **to betray** [bɪ'treɪ] verraten **tenderness** ['tendənəs] Zärtlichkeit **clasped** [klɑːspt] verschränkt **to thump** [θʌmp] pochen

"Mlle. Duhamel, would you consider being my friend?" Lucien asked, more seriously, he realized **abashedly**, than most men ask women to be their wives. "Would you consider friendship with a man who is sincere only at the core of his **ambiguous** heart and in the way he wishes to be a friend to you? A man whose very right hand is false?"

Mlle. Duhamel murmured **adoringly**, "I was just thinking that I held a hero's hand."

Lucien sat up a little. The words had taken him completely by surprise. "A hero's hand," he said sarcastically, but not without **contentment**.

---

abashedly [ə'bæʃtlɪ] beschämt **ambiguous** [æm'bɪgjʊəs] zweideutig, zwiegespalten **adoring** [ə'dɔːrɪŋ] bewundernd **contentment** [kən'tentmənt] Zufriedenheit

The Car

"I had Carlos wash the car today," Nicky said as he sat down at the table.

"I saw it. It looks beautiful." **Covertly**, she removed a **bewildered** ant from the tablecloth. "It was sweet of you to remember."

"Oh, you'll find I have a very good memory."

They smiled at each other, a little shyly, and with the **intent concern** of **newlyweds**. Actually, they had been married a year, but they thought of these last two weeks as their real **honeymoon**. In the last year, their marriage had been a matter of his flying up to San Francisco on rare weekends to see her, and of her going down to Mexico for the summer to see him. But now Florence had given up her teaching job and had come to live with him in San Vicente.

"It's nice I can see the car from the **porch**," Florence remarked, as she did almost every evening.

She gazed below her, half across the town, at the parking lot behind the Hotel Estrella del Sud. The Estrella del Sud, the best hotel in town, was where she had been staying when she met Nicky a year and a half ago on her summer vacation. The **farthest** car of the three in the **lot**, the big aquamarine Pontiac, was hers. It was the first car she had ever owned. She had bought it with her own money, saved over a period of years. The car was more than a year old, but still looked brand-new, because she was **meticulous** about its weekly washing and she had never gotten a scratch on it.

"I wish you could drive it, too, Nicky."

"Oh, I don't mind. I'll enjoy it enough." He could not drive because of his weak eyes.

---

covertly ['kʌvətlı] heimlich **bewildered** [bı'wıldəd] verwirrt **intent** [ın'tent] aufmerksam **concern** [kən'sɜːn] Anteilnahme **newlyweds** ['njuːlıwedz] junges Ehepaar **honeymoon** ['hʌnımuːn] Flitterwochen **porch** [pɔːtʃ] Veranda **farthest** ['fɑːðıst] am weitesten entfernt **lot** [lɒt] Parkplatz **meticulous** [mə'tıkjələs] peinlich genau

"Have more soup, Nicky."

"No, thanks, I couldn't. It's awfully good, though."

She went into the kitchen and came back with a **platter** on which sat a well-browned roast surrounded by **braised** potatoes, carrots, and peas. She set it down modestly.

"Boy!" Nicky exclaimed, though he took little interest in food. "You're feeding me much too well, Florence."

"I got the roast yesterday in Mexico City. I wanted to surprise you."

"You certainly did." He began **carving**.

"The meat markets in this town are a sight, Nicky. They're so smelly, I can't even get through the door. I've decided once a week I'll drive to Mexico City for fresh butter and meat."

"The meat's not as bad as it looks, you know." He smiled at her as he sat down. "The natives look pretty healthy, don't they?"

Florence nodded agreeably. It was what he always said whenever she questioned the cleanliness of anything in Mexico. She gave a start, and under the table drew up one foot and **pinched** at her ankle. There was a **flea** inside her sock, but it was foolish to try to kill it by pinching, she knew, because only a pair of **thumbnails** were of any use. She could tell a flea easily from an ant now. Fleas moved in **stealthy jerks**, while ants went steadily in one direction, even if it was a wrong one. Compared to fleas, ants were innocent, friendly little creatures.

She helped Nicky to more and more food, despite his protestations, but otherwise they said little to each other. She listened to the tinkling music of the cantinas' **jukeboxes** that were starting up here and there with the fall of night. From the hill where they lived, they had a splendid view of pink-roofed houses spilling one atop the other down a hillside, of a small,

---

platter ['plætə] Servierplatte **braised** [breɪzd] geschmort **to carve** [kɑːv] Fleisch schneiden, tranchieren **to pinch** [pɪntʃ] zwicken, kratzen **flea** [fliː] Floh **thumbnail** ['θʌmneɪl] Daumennagel **stealthy** ['stelθɪ] verstohlen, *hier:* unerwartet **jerk** [dʒɜːk] Sprung, Satz **jukebox** ['dʒuːkbɒks] Musikbox

bushy valley just below where pigs and chickens wandered, of the dark green treetops in front of the cathedral's yellow towers, and finally of the mountains that lay in no **range** but loomed up everywhere, around the full circle of the horizon. She felt very happy here with Nicky.

"Would you like some more tea?" she asked when they were starting on the chocolate layer cake she had baked. Nicky did not drink coffee except in the mornings, and she had **adjusted** her habits to **suit** his.

"I would if it's **convenient**."

While she was in the kitchen, Nicky stood up and strolled to the balustrade of the porch. He was a slightly built man of about forty, hardly taller than Florence, of Belgian birth and Swiss and German **descent**. Usually his face had an expression of impersonal amiability, an expression sometimes seen on the faces of people whose business it is to be pleasant to everyone. He was manager of the second-best hotel in the town.

He put his **lean** hands on the porch **rail** and tested its **steadiness**. He had built the porch himself the week before Florence arrived. The two-room house he had rented would have been nothing without the porch. They were saving all the money they could to buy a house on the other side of the cathedral. The new house cost twelve thousand pesos in down payment, but they had forty-five thousand now, counting the four thousand dollars Florence was going to draw from her bank in the States. Nicky wanted very much to own a house, because he felt that no one was anything in San Vicente unless one did. He was looking forward to spending the rest of his life in a comfortable house with a comfortable wife.

---

range [reɪndʒ] Kette **to adjust** [ə'dʒʌst] angleichen **to suit** [suːt] (an)passen, entsprechen **convenient** [kən'viːnjənt] passend, genehm **descent** [dɪ'sent] Abstammung **lean** [liːn] schmal, schlank **rail** [reɪl] Reling, Brüstung **steadiness** ['stedinəs] Stabilität

"Nicky, what's the matter with the water?" Florence called to him. "It won't run."

Nicky came into the little **galley** of a kitchen. A thin trickle of water **wheezed** into the dishpan Florence held.

"I've been waiting a long time. It's on full force."

"Couldn't be the **drought** already," Nicky said, half to himself. "I guess it is the drought starting, all right. It's early yet—but we'd feel it first up here on the hill."

After a few days, the water stopped running in the daytime, but came on mysteriously for a few minutes around ten in the evening. Hearing it **belch** through the **taps** they had left open, Nicky and Florence would hurry and fill all the buckets and pans in the house. A week later, there was no more water at any time, and they were forced to **haul** it, pairs of buckets by pairs of buckets, from the nearest fountain, which was at the foot of the hill. The distance down to the fountain was only a few hundred yards, but the climb back made the **chore exhausting** and even dangerous. The **cobblestone** lane was **steep**, and it was a common thing to see people slip and take bad falls.

Since Nicky had little time to wait in line at the public fountain and Florence was rather weakened by diarrhea, they **hired** a woman to work half days for them. It was an extra **expense**, but under the circumstances a necessary one. Nicky knew they would have no water until June when the rains came, and this was only the middle of March.

In **saddle oxfords** and socks, a blouse and tweed skirt, Florence walked **self-consciously** past Pepe's Bar into the shade of the plaza's trees. She looked up at the open balcony of

---

galley ['gælɪ] *hier:* Küchenzeile **to wheeze** [wiːz] *hier:* tröpfeln **drought** [draʊt] Trockenheit **to belch** [beltʃ] gurgeln **tap** [tæp] Wasserhahn **to haul** [hɔːl] schleppen **chore** [tʃɔː] langweilige (Routine-) Arbeit **exhausting** [ɪg'zɔːstɪŋ] erschöpfend **cobblestone** ['kɒblstəʊn] Kopfsteinpflaster **steep** [stiːp] steil **to hire** ['haɪə] mieten, anstellen **expense** [ɪk'spens] Ausgabe **saddle oxfords** *Pl.* ['sædl ˌɒksfədz] geschnürte Lederhalbschuhe **self-consciously** [ˌself'kɒnʃəslɪ] unsicher

Pepe's, where the usual six o'clock crowd **jammed** the little tables. The balcony was bright with sports clothes, and through the **brassy din** of the four-piece Mexican band, she could catch American phrases.

"Oh, Freddie, you *didn't*!"

"I did! Lord knows what was in it, but I ate it!"

A shriek of laughter that could only be American laughter.

She longed to be up there with them, and yet she wondered if she would be happy even then. Nicky had taken her up to the balcony one evening, but he hadn't known anyone. "Oh, these are mostly new tourists," he had said. And all of them had been so much better dressed than they that Florence had felt **subdued** and uncomfortable. Besides, she didn't like to drink, not even beer.

She bought some peanuts in a newspaper **cornucopia** for fifty centavos, and took them to a bench. She broke the shells slowly, eating the nuts one at a time, watching the balcony with the **wistful** expression of a child who is there and yet not there, listening at the same time for the car that would come up the narrow street at the corner of the plaza. Nicky had taken the car yesterday with his friend Mr. Sigismundo to drive to Mexico City, as they both had business to do for the hotel. It was the first night she had spent alone in Mexico, and now she was eager for Nicky's return. The peanuts were nearly gone when she heard the familiar motor, and the change to first **gear** for the climb to the plaza's level.

"Nicky!" She stepped into the road and waved as the car crept toward her. Here was one thing she needn't feel ashamed of before the people on the balcony. Not many of them had a car as beautiful as hers.

"Hi, Florence!"

---

to jam [dʒæm] quetschen, pferchen **brassy** ['brɑːsɪ] blechern **din** [dɪn] Lärm **subdued** [səb'djuːd] unterlegen, nicht ebenbürtig **cornucopia** [ˌkɔːnjʊ'kəʊpɪə] Tüte **wistful** ['wɪstfl] sehnsüchtig **gear** [gɪə] Gang (Getriebe)

Florence started to open the door on Nicky's side, when she saw that the backseat was full of Mexicans. They were not Mexicans like Mr. Sigismundo, but Mexicans in sombreros and dirty shirts, four or five of them.

"It's all right. Get in." Nicky made room for her in front.

Then one of the Mexicans opened a rear door, and there was a **squawk** of chickens. One by one they got out, two with chickens' legs in each hand, one with a tiny white **goat** in his arms, and with bowing and tipping of hats they **bade their adieus** to Nicky and Alfredo.

"Adíos, señor! Muchas gracias!"

"Por nada! Adíos!—Adíos, señor!" Nicky smiled and nodded to each in turn.

"Who are they?" Florence asked.

"Oh, we picked them up this side of Puebla," Nicky replied. "How've you been?"

"All right." Florence twisted around, and inspected the back of the car. There was a **swipe** of mud on the edge of the seat, marks of dusty feet on the floor, a **blob** from a chicken. "Nicky, why'd you let them bring a *goat* in here?"

Nicky gave the backseat a glance. "Oh, I'll clean that, Florence."

"Did they **mess** it?" Alfredo Sigismundo asked. He pulled into the parking lot and stopped.

"Not much," Nicky said. *"Buena noche,* Carlos!" he called to the **caretaker**.

Florence didn't trust herself to speak until Alfredo left them. Then she said, "Nicky, promise me you'll never pick up people like that in my car again."

Nicky smiled. "Why, Florence, they were stuck on the road with a broken **cart axle**. You couldn't just pass them by."

---

squawk [skwɔːk] Kreischen **goat** [gəʊt] Ziege **bade** *Pret.* **to bid o.'s adieu** [beɪd] sich verabschieden **swipe** [swaɪp] Schmiere **blob** [blɒb] Klecks, Spritzer **to mess** [mes] schmutzig machen **caretaker** ['keəteɪkə] Hausmeister **cart axle** ['kɑːt æksl] Wagenachse

Florence sat **tensely** in the leather chair, her Spanish lesson book open on her lap, watching Maria, the cleaning woman, moving about on the porch. In a minute, Florence thought, Maria would come to the **threshold** and **jabber** something about going home, and at that instant something inside her was going to burst in a million pieces.

The woman moved more and more slowly, **idly** readjusted a plate, whisked an ant off the tablecloth, because everything was ready and had been for nearly an hour. But Nicky had not arrived. Florence knew he was in one of the cantinas, drinking beer, talking on and on with Mr. Sigismundo and a lot of other Mexicans. It was the fifth time he had been very late. The third time, she remembered, she had gone down to get him, but it had been an **embarrassing** experience. Women were not supposed to set foot in the ordinary cantinas, so she had stood in the street in front of the open door until Mr. Sigismundo had seen her and **poked** Nicky. Then she had moved into the shadow by the wall and waited until Nicky had come out. Nicky was never really drunk but he could get **tipsy** enough not to realize or care that he kept her waiting. What **annoyed** her most was that when he came home on such evenings, he would invite Maria and her dirty little daughter, if they were around, to have dinner with them. Imagine! Mexican help eating their good food at their own table!

She watched Maria seat herself on the porch rail and run her fingers through her long, loose hair. Florence would gladly have **dismissed** her for the day, but she was not sure of the Spanish, and besides, the woman's presence in the house somehow **paralyzed** her. Florence hated her. She had **haggled** forty-five pesos out of Nicky for half-time work, when fifty a

---

tensely ['tenslɪ] angespannt **threshold** ['θreʃhəʊld] (Tür-)Schwelle **to jabber** ['dʒæbə] plappern **idly** ['aɪdlɪ] träge **embarrassing** [ɪm'bærəsɪŋ] peinlich **to poke** [pəʊk] anstupsen **tipsy** ['tɪpsɪ] beschwipst **to annoy** [ə'nɔɪ] verärgern **to dismiss s.o.** [dɪs'mɪs] j-n entlassen **to paralyze** ['pærəlaɪz] lähmen **to haggle** ['hægl] feilschen, handeln

month was standard for full-time, she ate their food behind their backs and moreover was lazy and **deliberately neglectful** of the main thing she had been hired for—to see that there were always three or four buckets of water in the house. And when Florence could get Nicky to speak to her, she would say she hadn't been able to understand a thing that the *señora* told her to do. Just let a servant behave like that in the States and see what would happen!

Florence's face took on a childlike expression of **affront** as she gazed at Maria. Her face was round, good-natured, and naive. When she was pleased, it broke out in a small, upcurving, wooden-angel smile, and when she was surprised or hurt, these emotions were recorded, not promptly but **accurately**, in her face and even in her body. Now there was hardly a **trace** of lipstick on her thin, soft lips, and the powder she had put on an hour before had **vanished**. Her nose shone as it generally did with a kind of dead whiteness between **splotched** pink and white cheeks. She had gained weight from lack of exercise (in California she had played a lot of tennis), and there had grown about her an air of no longer caring, of having been **defeated**, as anyone might have been, by **privation** and primitive living. She looked older than thirty-one, and even by San Vicente's informal standards she was **dowdy**.

She twisted around to see the clock, but it was already too dark in the room. The chair creaked loudly as she moved. It was a **sprawling**, uncomfortable chair that Nicky had **inherited** from the hotel where he worked. Florence **suspected** they had got rid of it because it was full of fleas. The back and seat were made of one piece of leather, and though shaped invitingly, it was hard as a rock to sit on. A month ago, she had

---

deliberately [dɪ'lɪbərətlɪ] absichtlich **neglectful** [nɪ'glektfl] nachlässig **affront** [ə'frʌnt] Beleidigung, Kränkung **accurately** ['ækjʊrətlɪ] genau **trace** [treɪs] Spur **to vanish** ['vænɪʃ] verschwinden **splotched** ['splɒtʃt] gesprenkelt **defeated** [dɪ'fiːtɪd] geschlagen, besiegt **privation** [praɪ'veɪʃn] Entbehrung **dowdy** ['daʊdɪ] nachlässig gekleidet, schlampig **sprawling** ['sprɔːlɪŋ] *hier:* ausladend, groß **to inherit** [ɪn'herɪt] erben **to suspect** [sə'spekt] vermuten, argwöhnen

torn her last pair of silk **stockings** from the States on the rough edge of the leather. On that day, too, she remembered, she had waited for Nicky to come home to dinner, an especially good dinner, and he had not come until nearly midnight. She **swallowed**, as though to thrust back the memory of the miserable evening **lest** she start weeping and the woman see her. The woman was coming.

"All right, all right!" Florence interrupted.

The **torrent** of shrill, **complaining** words stopped abruptly.

Then, because her voice had been harsh, Florence said very courteously, with a smile and gestures toward the door, *"Sta beeyen, señora, sta mooey beeyen."*

With a final **shrug** and an amused little smile that Florence knew was at her bad accent, the woman **ambled off**.

She felt better as soon as the woman was gone. The house was all hers again. She no longer wanted to fling herself across the bed and weep, and she almost decided not to **scold** Nicky. She really hated **arguments**, and she had held her tongue many times so Nicky might not think he had married a **nagger**. She **slanted** her Spanish book toward the light and stared at a **declension chart** of irregular verbs.

"Concha!—*Concha!"*

It was Maria, calling her daughter in the street. Tomorrow she would tell Nicky she had stayed long overtime, and Nicky would pay her extra, though he would tell Florence that he hadn't. She had once thought Nicky **economical**, even a little **stingy**, but these two months had changed her mind. He spent

---

stockings ['stɒkɪŋz] Strümpfe **to swallow** ['swɒləʊ] schlucken **lest** [lest] damit nicht **torrent** ['tɒrənt] Schwall **complaining** [kəm'pleɪnɪŋ] klagend **shrug** [ʃrʌg] Achselzucken **to amble off** [ˌæmbl‿'ɒf] davonschlendern **to scold** [skəʊld] schimpfen **argument** ['ɑːgjʊmənt] Streit **nagger** ['nægə] Nörgler(in) **to slant** [slɑːnt] verschieben, schräg halten **declension chart** [dɪ'klenʃn tʃɑːt] Konjugationstabelle **economical** [ˌiːkə'nɒmɪkl] sparsam **stingy** ['stɪndʒɪ] geizig

at least seventy pesos a week on beer alone, and as far as she could see let himself be **cheated** by every tradesman in town.

The cathedral **chimes** struck, and she got up restlessly. She stood on one foot, debating whether to turn the light on, scratching flea bites on her **calf** with the **laces** of her shoe. She listened for Nicky's step, but all she heard were the street sounds that came with startling clarity from just behind the wall, the clatter of a **burro's** tiny **hooves**, Mexican men's voices drifting past in pairs and the **slap** of their sandals on the stones, the **whack** and **slide** of the boards the children rode like **sleds** down the hill, making the cobbles as **slick** as glass.

The **lane** beside the house was another thing wrong! It was not only the noisiest, busiest lane in town, but the steepest. She fell on it about twice a week, fell on her face or sat down hard, always amid giggles of children. In the dark, it was risking **life and limb** to use it unless one went backward on all fours. After **dusk**, she felt imprisoned in the house. Why they didn't put steps in, she couldn't see. There was enough picturesque about San Vicente without having lanes that broke people's necks.

Every direction her thoughts took led to the same **impasses** of **discomfort**. Nicky did not seem to realize how hard it was for her, how lonely it was without her friends, how much more **confining** it was in a Latin country for a woman than for a man. She had thought he would have a few American friends in the town, but all his friends seemed to be Mexicans. The time he had taken her to the Barreras' had been awful. They had tried to be nice, but neither the husband nor the

---

to cheat [tʃiːt] betrügen, schwindeln **chime** [tʃaɪm] Glockengeläute **calf** [kɑːf] Wade **lace** [leɪs] Schuhband **burro** ['bʊrəʊ] kleiner Esel **hooves** *Pl.* **hoof** [huːvz] Huf **slap** [slæp] Klatschen **whack** [wæk] knallender Schlag **slide** [slaɪd] Gleiten, Rutschen **sled** *i.e.* **sledge** [sled, sledʒ] Schlitten **slick** [slɪk] glatt, rutschig **lane** [leɪn] Gasse **life and limb** [ˌlaɪf ən 'lɪm] Kopf und Kragen **dusk** [dʌsk] Dämmerung **impasse** [æm'pɑːs] Sackgasse **discomfort** [dɪs'kʌmfət] Unbequemlichkeit, Unbehagen **confining** [kən'faɪnɪŋ] beengend, beschränkend

wife had known any English, and she had sat through the whole evening not understanding a word, keeping a pleasant expression on her face until she felt like a **ninny**.

She walked slowly through the foyer and onto the porch. The light from the Estrella del Sud's dining room fell on the parking lot behind it. She stared at her car and felt better, though the tears rose in her eyes until the **twinkles** of the rear **bumper** looked like stars with long points. Often when she was lonely or depressed, she would look at her car for long moments, while all sorts of things ran in her mind, thoughts of home, the voices of her mother and her brother and sisters saying things she had heard them say and had not known she remembered. She would think of the places she had been to in the car last summer with her sister Clara. Yellowstone Park and the **geysers**. The Black Hills of South Dakota. The roadstands where they had stopped for hamburgers and Cokes. Good American hamburgers, served in clean paper **napkins** fastened with a **toothpick**. ...

There was a **thump** on the door, followed by three **facetious** little **raps**, and she wiped her eyes and mechanically pushed her hair into place before she went to the door and opened it.

"Hello. I forgot my keys," Nicky said, smiling as he came in. His small blue eyes blinked **affably**, but the lids were pink and swollen as they always were after he had been drinking. "Sorry I'm late."

"Oh, that's all right," Florence replied in an expressionless voice, for at the last minute she had not been able to decide whether to be angry, cool, or to overlook.

Nicky, assured that she was not **vexed** with him, opened the door again. "Come on in."

---

ninny ['nɪnɪ] Dussel, Dummkopf **twinkle** ['twɪŋkl] Blitzen, Funkeln **bumper** ['bʌmpə] Stoßstange **geyser** ['giːzə] Geysir, *heiße Springquelle in vulkanischer Erde* **napkin** ['næpkɪn] Serviette **toothpick** ['tuːθpɪk] Zahnstocher **thump** [θʌmp] dumpfer Schlag **facetious** [fə'siːʃəs] witzig, spaßig **rap** [ræp] Klopfen **affably** ['æfəblɪ] leutselig **vexed** [vekst] böse, verärgert

Alfredo Sigismundo's aristocratic figure **descended** the two steps into the foyer. Florence smelt the thin, medicinal aroma of tequila as he bent low over her hand and **deposited** a **moist** kiss.

"Ha! Ha!" Nicky laughed, as though both he and Alfredo considered this Latin courtesy a great joke. "You don't mind if Alfredo joins us for dinner, do you, Florence?"

"Why, no."

Alfredo passed a finger over his small black mustache. "Just a moment," his voice vibrated richly, "till I wash my hands." He took two careful **strides** on tiptoe before his hand went out to support him on a **doorjamb**. One **starched** white **cuff** glowed in the half darkness.

"Oh, there isn't any water in there, Mr. Sigismundo," Florence said, finding her tongue suddenly. She **fumbled** for the light string in the kitchen, and remembered with sudden pain that the toilet had not been **flushed** since that morning. "Nicky!" Florence called. She found the light string. Only one bucket of the six held water. The woman had not brought *any* that day. Florence felt ready to cry. "Here, Nicky!" she whispered, thrusting the full bucket into his hands. "Go flush the toilet!"

"Oh, he understands how things are with the drought on," Nicky said with **elaborate reassurance**.

"Go flush it! Hurry!"

"All right," he whispered back, and went.

Florence, her breath held in shame, walked onto the porch. Then, reminded by the sight of the table, she quickly laid another place and brought a chair from the kitchen. She lighted fires under all the pots, started to put water on for tea, then remembered the water was in the bathroom.

---

to descend [dɪ'send] herabsteigen **to deposit** [dɪ'pɒzɪt] ablegen, -setzen **moist** [mɔɪst] feucht **stride** [straɪd] Schritt **doorjamb** ['dɔːdʒæm] Türrahmen **starched** [stɑːtʃt] steif, gestärkt **cuff** [kʌf] Manschette **to fumble** ['fʌmbl] tastend suchen **to flush (the toilet)** [flʌʃ, 'tɔɪlət] (die Toilette) spülen **elaborate** [ɪ'læbərət] sorgfältig, überlegt **reassurance** [ˌriːə'ʃʊərəns] Beruhigung

"Don't we have any beer?" Nicky called with his head in the **icebox**. "Ah, here's some."

"Nicky!" She came and **grasped** his arm. "Don't let him use all that water. It's all we have for tea."

"Oh," Nicky said, and started off to the bathroom, where Alfredo was singing to himself in a soft baritone.

Florence seized a saucepan and with a hope that never died turned on the **faucet**. Nothing happened. Not even a wheeze.

"Here it is." Nicky presented her with the bucket in which less than two inches of water remained.

Florence said nothing. She was too near tears.

When Alfredo came back, Nicky said casually, "I thought I might take the car tomorrow, Florence. Alfredo wants to go to Mexico City, and I've got to go anyway to get somebody's typewriter repaired."

"Whose typewriter?" Florence asked **vaguely**.

"A fellow's who's staying at the hotel. He's a writer and he needs it right away."

"Won't you sit down, Mr. Sigismundo?" Florence **gestured** toward the table and **ducked** into the kitchen.

She brought the big **china tureen** to the table, and Alfredo dragged himself up from his chair. He bowed deeply, an unlighted American cigarette hanging from his lips.

"Oh, please don't get up," Florence said, flattered and laughing a little in spite of herself.

"All right, Florence?" Nicky asked.

"What?"

"If we take the car tomorrow."

"Oh." She looked from him to Mr. Sigismundo, who **exhaled** a long stream of smoke and stared tiredly into the distance before him. "Well—all right, Nicky. Of course."

---

icebox ['aɪsbɒks] Kühlschrank **to grasp** [grɑːsp] packen **faucet** ['fɔːsɪt] Wasserhahn **vaguely** ['veɪglɪ] unbestimmt **to gesture** ['dʒestʃə] zeigen auf **to duck** [dʌk] sich davonmachen **china tureen** ['tʃaɪnə təˌriːn] Porzellanterrine **to exhale** [eks'heɪl] ausatmen

Nicky leaned over and laid a hand on Alfredo's shoulder. "See?"

Florence smiled and nodded awkwardly to Mr. Sigismundo as she sat down, for once more he had stood up and bowed, though without looking at her. She had a frozen smile on her lips and it would remain as long as Mr. Sigismundo was in her house. She felt his eyes fixed seriously on the soup as she **la-dled it** into the bowls. She knew he would not say a word to her during the meal, that afterward he and Nicky would sit on the porch talking Spanish until the beer was gone, and then go down the hill to a cantina.

"I don't know what's happened to the car," Nicky said, his voice as calm as ever. "Probably nothing's happened to it at all. Alfredo's a very good driver, you know."

"But—two days ago, you said. Where was he going?"

"I don't know." Nicky removed his leather jacket slowly. "We were both taking a **nap** in our hotel room about three o'-clock, and Alfredo woke me up and said he was going out to visit a friend near Chapultepec."

"Where's that?"

"Oh, that's right in Mexico City. You remember Chapulte-pec Castle. Where Maximilian and Carlotta lived."

"Didn't you *look* for the car?"

Nicky opened his hands **gently**. "There's not much use looking for it in a big city, Florence. I wouldn't worry. He'll probably come in with it today." He took his shaving articles out of his **valise**.

"Oh!" Florence gasped, on the edge of tears. "I just can't un-derstand you, Nicky. I can't—Why you even **lower yourself** to associate with him, I can't understand!"

Nicky blinked at her. "These things just happen in Mexico,"

---

to ladle ['leɪdl] (Suppe etc.) schöpfen **nap** [næp] Nickerchen **gently** ['dʒentlɪ] freundlich **valise** [və'li:z] Reisetasche **to lower o.s.** ['ləʊə] sich erniedrigen

he said **soothingly**. "Don't forget you're dealing with a different kind of people from Americans."

"I don't forget it! How can I forget it, when you're getting just as **shiftless** as they are!"

Nicky **trailed** her onto the porch. She was looking down on the parking lot, at the **gap** where her car had stood. "You've no right to say that, Florence. I just meant—"

"Don't talk to me about rights. You had no right to ask for my car and give it to that **lowlifer**."

"Why, I wouldn't call Alfredo that."

"I would. He keeps mistresses. I've heard of his affairs right inside the hotel, and I've heard about his women in Mexico City, too. And now he's probably given my *car* to one of them!" She bent forward and ran with her hands over her face into the bedroom. She cried for several minutes on the bed. Then, when Nicky came out of the bathroom in a clean shirt, freshly shaven, his thin brown hair slicked down with water, she sat up and wiped the tears out of her eyes. "Would you like some breakfast?"

Nicky looked at his watch. "Lunch is more like it."

"Will **scrambled eggs** be all right? It'll be a long time before Maria comes with the **groceries**."

"That's fine, Florence." Nicky ran his thumb under the **wrapper** of his new *Time,* stretched out on the bed, and began to read.

"I was over to look at the house again," Nicky said when he came home that evening. "There's a fellow from Mexico City in the hotel who knows about **plumbing**, so we went over. He said it wouldn't cost more than six hundred pesos to make

---

soothingly ['suːðɪŋglɪ] beruhigend **shiftless** ['ʃɪftləs] träge, faul **to trail s.o.** [treɪl] j-m nachgehen, folgen **gap** [gæp] Lücke **lowlifer** ['ləʊlaɪfə] zwielichtiger Typ **scrambled eggs** [ˌskræmbld 'egz] Rührei **groceries** *Pl.* ['grəʊsərɪz] Lebensmittel **wrapper** ['ræpə] Umschlag **plumbing** ['plʌmɪŋ] Klempnerarbeit

those repairs on the bathroom. That's about half what we'd **figured**, you know."

Florence gazed at him **dully**. Her face was shiny and tear-swollen.

Nicky talked on and on, **oblivious of** her expression. He was not clever in perceiving people's **moods**. In his business, he was used to sizing people up as easily pleased, **irascible**, or something in between, and he knew Florence belonged in the first category. If he noticed the despair on her face, he thought to himself, "Oh, she's worried about the car, but I've already told her it'll turn up." So he talked on, until one of her **sniffles** was so loud it interrupted him.

"I'll not buy that house with *my* good money!" she said so suddenly that he jumped.

He stood up in alarm.

"I don't want to live here! I don't want to own land here! You just want me to sink my hard-earned money in property so I'll **be anchored** here, that's all. You want the car to get stolen, too, so I can't leave. But I'll show you!" She flung the sentences at him **defiantly** but a little fearfully, as a child might at an unjust governor.

Nicky turned half-away, undecided. It was as if a **gale** had blown through him, **ruffling** his **tranquil** inner being. He did not for an instant believe her **threats**. It was only her **vehemence** that shocked him. He was angrier than he had ever been in his life as he lifted his jacket from the hook, put it on, and went out.

Florence spent the rest of the evening weeping and writing a letter to her mother.

---

to figure ['fɪgə] sich vorstellen **dully** ['dʌlɪ] teilnahmslos **oblivious of** [ə'blɪvɪəs] ohne zu achten auf **mood** [mu:d] Laune, Stimmung **irascible** [ɪ'ræsəbl] jähzornig **sniffle** ['snɪfl] Schniefen **to be anchored** ['æŋkəd] angehängt, festgelegt sein **defiantly** [dɪ'faɪəntlɪ] herausfordernd **gale** [geɪl] Sturm **to ruffle** ['rʌfl] aufwühlen **tranquil** ['træŋkwɪl] ruhig, besonnen **threat** [θret] Drohung **vehemence** ['vi:əməns] Heftigkeit

April 24th

Dearest Mama,

Something terrible has happened. Nicky borrowed my car to go to Mexico City with Mr. Sigismundo and Mr. Sigismundo has just kept it. This was three days ago. Nicky thinks he will bring the car back, but I don't. I think he has stolen it. I don't ***trust*** *Mexicans one inch and for all his manners and education Mr. Sigismundo is still a Mexican.*

Added to all this, life still isn't very pleasant down here. The drought is still on and will be for six more weeks. They are building a ***dam*** *in the mountains to* ***ensure*** *a water system (****supply****) all year, but it will be two more years before it is finished. I can't tell you how it is not to have water in the house. You have to go through it to know. Everything seems to be dirty all the time and finally you just accept it and live like a pig.*

Mama, I am tired tonight and can't say things very well, but I must tell you that I don't think I can stand it down here much longer. Nicky can because he is used to it, but I just can't. If I come home, it means leaving Nicky down here, because he won't come to the States to live. He thinks he cannot make the ***grade*** *in American hotels and I can't even get him to try. I don't want you to think it is because Nicky and I are not getting along. He is very easy to get along with and is a fine husband. It is just the country I can't stand. I haven't even talked to Nicky yet about it, but I wanted to explain to you if I could. I'll write you soon when I decide something.*

Ever your loving daughter,
Florence

P.S. My love to Clara and Ben and the kids. Most of all to you.

She put the letter in her top drawer under a stack of **handkerchiefs**, then fell into bed.

When she awoke, it was bright day. Sunshine fell through the single window onto the bed, onto the **heap** of dirty stock-

---

to trust [trʌst] vertrauen **dam** [dæm] Damm **to ensure** [en'ʃʊə] sicherstellen **supply** [sə'plaɪ] Vorrat **grade** [greɪd] Grad, Stufe, Abschluss e-r Ausbildung **handkerchief** ['hæŋkətʃɪf] Taschentuch **heap** [hiːp] Haufen

ings, socks, and underwear that was collecting beside the bathroom door, onto her dry, dirty-nailed hands that she spread on the coverlet and looked at miserably. She had a headache and a bad taste in her mouth. She had not washed last night, because there was no water, and of course there was none now. She remembered last night, remembered her letter and her decision. Nicky had not come home. She supposed he had slept at the hotel. Tonight she would get things settled with him in a civilized way, and leave as soon as she could.

She drew on a **bathrobe**. She felt strangely relaxed and free already. Her feet padded across the tiles until her thighs struck the rail of the porch. Through old habit her eyes **strayed** to the parking lot.

There she saw—with an astonishment that shocked and thrilled her—her car in its usual place! She leaned far over the rail, not yet believing her eyes, but there was no mistake. It was a miracle that had happened in the night!

She got dressed as fast as she could, hurried without fear or **mishap** down the hill and up to the parking lot. She touched one of the shining **fenders**. She wanted to laugh and cry at the same time. Then she trotted up the ramp and entered the Estrella del Sud's lobby before she remembered that after last night's **quarrel**, she ought not to call Nicky. But she was so happy, she could not control herself. She had to tell someone, and there was no one but Nicky. She went into a **booth** and dialed the number of Nicky's hotel.

"Está el Señor Spangli?" she asked, even taking pleasure in her Spanish.

A **spate** of Spanish came back at her, then silence, and she **assumed** they were calling him.

Finally Nicky's voice said, *"Bueno?"*

"Nicky, the car's back! It's in the parking lot!"

---

bathrobe ['bɑːθrəʊb] Morgenmantel **to stray** [streɪ] wandern **mishap** ['mɪshæp] Missgeschick **fender** ['fendə] Kotflügel **quarrel** ['kwɒrəl] Streit **booth** [buːð] Telefonzelle **spate** [speɪt] Wortschwall **to assume** [ə'sjuːm] annehmen

"I know," Nicky said with a little laugh. "Alfredo got in early this morning."

"I'm so glad it's back!"

"Yes. So am I. He said he **was delayed** because one of his relatives died and he had to go to the funeral."

"Oh.—Are you feeling all right, Nicky?"

"I guess so. A little headache." He laughed again, **apologetically**. "I've got to go now, Florence. Someone's calling me."

She walked home **rejoicing** in her heart. Even as she climbed the hill, her **thighs aching**, her breath short, she felt she could **endure** the drought and make the best of things. How could she have thought of leaving Nicky! There never had been a **divorce** in her family, and it would have hurt her mother terribly if she had caused the first. The car was back! And she would never, never let Mr. Sigismundo use it again.

At the top of the hill, she remembered there was no water. She got two buckets from the house and went down the hill again.

The very next day, Florence fell down in the lane and **bruised** one knee severely. It gave her **agonizing** pain, and the doctor Nicky called in said she would have to spend two weeks or more in bed. The knee swelled to frightening size and turned black, purple, brown, and finally a **mottled** yellow. Nicky tried to **comfort** her by telling her that **injuries** always swelled in tropical countries and were not so bad as they seemed. Then during the second week in bed another accident

---

to be delayed [dɪˈleɪd] aufgehalten werden **apologetically** [əˌpɒləˈdʒetɪklɪ] entschuldigend **to rejoice** [rɪˈdʒɔɪs] frohlocken **thigh** [θaɪ] Oberschenkel **to ache** [eɪk] wehtun **to endure** [ɪnˈdjʊə] ertragen, aushalten **divorce** [dɪˈvɔːs] Scheidung **to bruise** [bruːz] prellen **agonizing** [ˈægənaɪzɪŋ] quälend **mottled** [ˈmɒtld] gefleckt **to comfort** [ˈkʌmfət] trösten **injury** [ˈɪndʒərɪ] Verletzung

befell her: something **stung** her over her left eye. She was sure it was the scorpion that lived in the **crack** in the wall just over the bed. The doctor **corroborated** her. It was a scorpion bite. The eye also swelled to great size and finally closed, except for a slit she could manage toward evening. The eye, too, went through a **weird** color cycle, but remained **predominantly** purple.

With the pain, her ugliness, and the inability to wash, the last **ounce** of morale left her. She suffered fever and **anguish** part of the day, and terrifying apathy the rest. At night she either could not sleep for pain or was too tired of bed to sleep. Nicky brought her **bougainvilleas** from the hotel garden, **candy** from the shop near the cathedral, but most of his evenings he spent in the cantinas. Florence did not **blame** him now. Lying there, thinking, she came to realize that there was not much else to do in San Vicente but drink, which was what almost everybody did. She tried to be thankful that Nicky drank only beer and not tequila. She had seen enough to know that in San Vicente **drunkard** husbands were crosses that many Mexican women and many American women had to bear.

She did not have the energy now to think of leaving. She lay in the state between sleeping and waking that **is astir with** fantastic dreams, and that finally makes a dream of reality. She believed herself nearer to death than ever before in her life. When she imagined she might die, she thought of leaving the car, her only **legacy**, and saw it **battered** and destroyed under Nicky's ownership. Then she would realize she was not dead

---

stung *Pret.* **to sting** [stʌŋ, stɪŋ] stechen **crack** [kræk] Ritze, Spalte **to corroborate** [kə'rɒbəreɪt] bestärken, bestätigen **weird** [wɪəd] unheimlich **predominantly** [prɪ'dɒmɪnəntlɪ] vorwiegend **ounce** [aʊns] Unze **anguish** ['æŋgwɪʃ] Angst **bougainvillea** [ˌbuːgən'vɪlɪə] *e-e purpurrot blühende Blumensorte* **candy** ['kændɪ] Süßigkeiten **to blame s.o.** [bleɪm] j-m e-n Vorwurf machen **drunkard** ['drʌŋkəd] Säufer **to be astir with** [ə'stɜː] wimmeln von **legacy** ['legəsɪ] Vermächtnis **battered** ['bætəd] verbeult

yet, that the car was waiting for her, that someday she might get in it and go north. But most of the time she had no desire to do anything or go anywhere. She had not the energy to hold a **mirror** and **comb** her hair. Above all, she did not want to see her face.

It was on one of the nights in the second week of her illness that Nicky came in about midnight, his eyes pink with drinking. He announced that he and Alfredo and some friends had decided to go to Mexico City to see a bullfight the next day, and that they would need the car.

Florence had awakened from **nightmarish** half sleep, and she was **propped** on one elbow, watching **dazedly** with her good eye as he packed his valise.

"I know you don't like bullfights," he said. "We'll be back day after tomorrow **without fail**. Alfredo, prince of drivers, will drive us."

"No," she said, and her voice **quavered** foolishly.

Nicky straightened and looked at her. "Florence, don't get excited."

Florence had a vision of the cantina Nicky had just left, of Nicky treating the house to beers and tequilas and then **expansively** inviting everyone to go to Mexico City in the car he would provide. She saw the drunken, unshaven Mexican men greeting his proposal with **drooling** shouts. "Don't take the car."

"I swear to you we'll be careful," Nicky said patiently. He sat on the edge of her bed and stretched his hands toward her shoulders, but she twisted away and got out on the other side.

---

mirror ['mɪrə] Spiegel **to comb** [kəʊm] kämmen **nightmarish** ['naɪtmeərɪʃ] alptraumhaft **propped** ['prɒpt] aufgestützt **dazedly** ['deɪzɪdlɪ] benommen, betäubt **without fail** [wɪˌðaʊt 'feɪl] ganz bestimmt **to quaver** ['kweɪvə] zittern **expansively** [ɪk'spænsɪvlɪ] großzügig **drooling** ['druːlɪŋ] begeistert

She slipped into her shoes and **hobbled** to the bureau where the keys were. Then she went to the closet and took a tweed coat off a **hanger**.

Nicky stood up slowly. "Really, Florence, you shouldn't be out of bed."

She did not waste energy in replying. She felt **nauseous** and weak, and she was afraid if she did not keep moving fast, she might **faint**. She got up the steps to the door, **slammed** it behind her and **plunged** recklessly down the hill.

She held her breath and let herself go, bending the **tortured** knee, taking fast little steps that kept her just ahead of **gravity**, feeling the same terror she had felt once when someone pushed her off a high **diving board**. The night was moonless and **pitch-black**, and her good eye, wildly stretched open, stared at her feet and saw absolutely nothing. She **slipped**, went down on one hand and pushed up again, **hurling herself onward**, because she felt that Nicky would come running down any second behind her. Suddenly she felt the road drop as though she had walked off the **edge** of something. She fell on her side and rolled over twice before her **sprawling** arms could stop her. She got to her feet, **trembling**. The ground was **level** now, and by the bus station's lamp she could see where she was, all the way at the foot of the hill, near the fountain that was growing clearer to her eye.

She ran for the parking lot. No one was about, and she felt she was **enacting** one of her dreams. She climbed into the front seat with her coat all **bunched** under her, zoomed the car back, and shot out the gate. She felt strong in the car. Its

---

to hobble ['hɒbl] humpeln **hanger** ['hæŋə] Kleiderbügel **nauseous** ['nɔːzɪəs] übel **to faint** [feɪnt] in Ohnmacht fallen **to slam** [slæm] zuschlagen **to plunge** [plʌndʒ] sich stürzen **tortured** ['tɔːtʃəd] schmerzhaft **gravity** ['grævətɪ] Schwerkraft **diving board** ['daɪvɪŋ bɔːd] Sprungbrett **pitch-black** [ˌpɪtʃ'blæk] rabenschwarz **to slip** [slɪp] ausrutschen **to hurl o.s. onward** [ˌhɜːl 'ɒnwəd] sich weiterschleppen **edge** [edʒ] Rand **sprawling** ['sprɔːlɪŋ] ausgestreckt **trembling** ['tremblɪŋ] zitternd **level** ['levl] eben **to enact** [ɪ'nækt] (nach-)spielen, wirklich werden lassen **to bunch** [bʌntʃ] zusammenraffen

power was unlimited, far more than she needed. She heard Nicky calling her name out of the darkness of the hill. Passing the plaza, she had a glimpse of Mr. Sigismundo's tall figure rising from a bench under one of the lampposts. There was a woman on the bench also.

Now she was out of the town. The wind came strong and clean through the open window, and the **tar** highway **hissed** under the **tires**. Her eyes, one wide, the other a slit in a **mound** of purple and yellow, watched the road at the farthest reach of the **headlights**. It was a two-lane road that wound around mountainside after mountainside in a general westward direction toward Mexico City. After Mexico City, she would go north on the road to Juarez. She pressed the pedal to the floor and the car leapt like a fish, took a long hill at a smoothly **increasing** speed, turned abruptly and began another climb.

Then, at a curve to the left, the car leaned in the opposite direction, going too fast for the turn it had to make. The **rubber shrieked** at Florence's sharp turning, the wheels on the right side struck **gravel**, dropped, and then the car shot over the edge and began to fall. It turned over and over, bumping down the mountainside with Florence inside it, and burst into flame before it quite came to a stop in the valley.

---

tar [tɑː] Teer, Asphalt **to hiss** [hɪs] zischen **tire** [taɪə] Reifen **mound** [maʊnd] *hier:* Schwellung **headlight** ['hedlaɪt] Scheinwerferlicht **increasing** [ɪn'kriːsɪŋ] zunehmend **rubber** ['rʌbə] Gummi **to shriek** [ʃriːk] quietschen **gravel** ['grævl] Kies

Quiet Night

Hattie pulled the little chain of the reading lamp, drew the covers over her shoulders, and lay **tense**, listening till Alice's sniffs and coughs should **subside**.

"Alice," she whispered.

No response. Yes, she was sleeping already, though she **insisted** she never closed an eye before the clock struck eleven.

Hattie eased herself to the edge of the bed, slowly put out a white **stockinged** foot. She **twisted** around to look at Alice, of whom nothing was visible except a thin nose **projecting** between the **ruffle** of her nightcap and the sheet pulled over her mouth. She was quite still.

Hattie rose **gently** from the bed, her breath coming short with excitement. In the **semidarkness** she could see the two sets of false teeth sitting in their glasses of water on the bed table. She **giggled** nervously.

Like a white ghost she made her way across the room, past the Victorian **upholstered settee**. She stopped at the **sewing table**, lifted the **folding top**, and **groped** among the **spools** and **pattern papers** till she found the cold metal of the scissors. Then holding them **tightly**, she crossed the room again. She had left the door of the **closet** slightly **ajar** earlier in the evening, and it swung open noiselessly. Hattie reached a **trembling** hand into the blackness, felt the two stiff woolen coats, a few dresses. Finally she touched a **fuzzy** thing hanging next to the wall. She

---

tense [tens] angespannt **to subside** [səb'saɪd] nachlassen **to insist** [ɪn'sɪst] behaupten **stockinged** ['stɒkɪŋd] bestrumpft **to twist** [twɪst] sich drehen **projecting** [prə'dʒektɪŋ] hervorstehend **ruffle** ['rʌfl] Rüsche **gently** ['dʒentlɪ] vorsichtig **semidarkness** [ˌsemɪ'dɑːknəs] Halbdunkel **to giggle** ['gɪgl] kichern **upholstered** [ʌp'həʊlstəd] gepolstert **settee** [se'tiː] Sofa **sewing table** ['səʊɪŋ teɪbl] Nähtisch **folding top** ['fəʊldɪŋ tɒp] Klappdeckel **to grope** [grəʊp] tastend suchen **spool** [spuːl] Spule **pattern paper** ['pætn peɪpə] Schnittmuster **tightly** ['taɪtlɪ] fest **closet** ['klɒzɪt] Schrank **ajar** [ə'dʒɑː] angelehnt **trembling** ['tremblɪŋ] zitternd **fuzzy** ['fʌzɪ] pelzig, weich

was giggling as she lifted the **hanger** down, and the scissors slipped out of her hand. There was a loud **clatter**, followed by some **half-suppressed** laughter. Hattie **peeked** round the door at Alice, motionless on the bed. Alice was rather **hard of hearing**.

With her white toes turned up stiffly, Hattie **clumped** to the easy chair by the window where a bar of moonlight **slanted**, and sat down with the scissors and the Angora sweater in her lap. In the moonlight her face **gleamed**, toothless and demoniacal. She examined the sweater in the manner of a person who plays with a piece of steak with a fork before deciding where to put his knife.

It was really a beautiful sweater. Alice had received it the week before from her niece. It was a birthday present, for Alice would never have **indulged in** such a luxury herself. She was happy as a child with it, and had worn it every day with her dresses.

The scissors cut **purringly** up the soft wool **sleeves**, between the **wristband** and the shoulder. She considered. There should be one more cut. The back, of course. But only about a foot long so it should not be immediately visible.

A few seconds later, she had put the scissors back into the table, hung the sweater in the closet, and was lying between the two feather mattresses. She **heaved a tremendous sigh.** She thought of the **gaping** sleeves, of Alice's face the next morning. The sweater was **utterly beyond repair** and she was immensely pleased with herself.

---

hanger ['hæŋə] Kleiderbügel **clatter** ['klætə] Klappern, Schepper **half-suppressed** [ˌhɑːfsə'prest] halb unterdrückt **to peek** [piːk] spähen **hard of hearing** [ˌhɑːd əv 'hɪərɪŋ] schwerhörig **to clump** [klʌmp] trampeln **to slant** [slɑːnt] schräg einfallen **to gleam** [gliːm] leuchten **to indulge in s.th.** [ɪn'dʌldʒ] sich etw. gönnen **purringly** ['pɜːrɪŋlɪ] schnurrend **sleeve** [sliːv] Ärmel **wristband** ['rɪstbænd] Bündchen **to heave a tremendous sigh** [ˌhiːv ə trəˌmendəs 'saɪ] einen tiefen Seufzer tun **gaping** ['geɪpɪŋ] klaffend **utterly** ['ʌtəlɪ] völlig **beyond repair** [bɪˌjɒnd rɪ'peə] nicht mehr zu flicken

They were awakened at eight-thirty by the hotel maid. It was a ritual that never failed: three **bony raps** on the door and a **bawling** voice, with a hint of **insolence**: "Eight-thirty. You can get breakfast now." Then Hattie, who always woke first, would **poke** Alice's shoulder.

Mechanically they sat up on their respective sides of the bed and pulled their nightgowns over their heads, **revealing** clean white undergarments. They said nothing. Five years of coexistence had **dwindled** their conversation to **rock-bottom efficiency**.

This morning, however, Hattie was thinking of the sweater. She felt **self-conscious**, but she could think of nothing to say or do to **relieve** the tension. Hattie spent some fifteen minutes doing her hair. She had a **braid** nearly two feet long when she fixed it at night, and twice a day she would take it down for its hundred **strokes**. Her hair was her only **vanity**. Already dressed, she stood shifting uneasily, pretending to be fastening her **snaps**.

But Alice seemed to **take an age** at the wash basin, gargling with her solution of salt and **tepid** water. She held **stubbornly** to salt and water in the morning, in spite of Hattie's **tempting** bottle of red mouthwash sitting on the shelf.

"What are you giggling at now?" Alice turned from the basin, her face wet and smiling a little. Hattie could say nothing, looked at the teeth in the glass and snickered again.

"Here's your teeth." She reached the glass **awkwardly** to Alice. "I thought you were going down to breakfast without them."

---

bony ['bəʊnɪ] knöchern **rap** [ræp] Klopfen **bawling** ['bɔːlɪŋ] brüllend **insolence** ['ɪnsələns] Unverschämtheit **to poke** [pəʊk] anstupsen **to reveal** [rɪ'viːl] enthüllen **to dwindle** ['dwɪndl] reduzieren **rock-bottom efficiency** [ˌrɒkˌbɒtəm ɪ'fɪʃnsɪ] das Allernötigste **self-conscious** [ˌself'kɒnʃəs] unsicher **to relieve** [rɪ'liːv] lindern **braid** [breɪd] Zopf **stroke** [strəʊk] Bürstenstrich **vanity** ['vænətɪ] Eitelkeit **snap** [snæp] Druckknopf **to take an age** [eɪdʒ] ewig lang brauchen **tepid** ['tepɪd] lauwarm **stubbornly** ['stʌbənlɪ] stur **tempting** ['temptɪŋ] verführerisch **awkwardly** ['ɔːkwədlɪ] ungeschickt

"Now when did I ever go off without my teeth, Hattie?"

Alice smiled **in spite of herself**. It was going to be a good day, she thought. Mrs. Crumm and her sister were back from a weekend, and they could all play **rummy** together in the afternoon. She walked to the closet in her stocking feet, a smile playing absently about her mouth.

Hattie watched as she took down the powder blue dress, the one that went best with the beige Angora. She fastened all the little buttons in front. She took the sweater off the hanger and put one arm into the sleeve.

"Oh," she breathed painfully. Then like a hurt child her eyes **squinted** and her face twisted **petulantly**. Tears came quickly down her cheeks. "H-Hattie ..." She turned to her and could say nothing else.

Hattie **smirked**, uncomfortable yet enjoying herself thoroughly. "Well I do know!" she exclaimed. "Who might have done a trick like that!" She went to the bed and sat down, doubled up with laughter.

"Hattie ... Hattie you did this," Alice declared in unsteady tones. She **clutched** the sweater to her. "Hattie ... you're just **mean**."

Lying across the bed, Hattie was almost hysterical. "You know I didn't now, Alice... . Hah-haw! ... Why do you think I'd ... ?" Her voice was **choked off** with uncontrolled laughter.

She lay there several minutes before she was calm enough to go down to breakfast. And when she left the room, Alice was sitting in the big chair by the window, **sobbing**, her face buried in the Angora sweater.

---

in spite of herself [spaɪt] unwillkürlich **rummy** ['rʌmɪ] Rommé *(Kartenspiel)* **to squint** [skwɪnt] blinzeln **petulantly** ['petjʊləntlɪ] bockig, trotzig **to smirk** [smɜːk] grinsen **to clutch** [klʌtʃ] klammern **mean** [miːn] gemein **to choke off** [tʃəʊk 'ɒf] ersticken **sobbing** ['sɒbɪŋ] schluchzend

Alice did not come down until she was called for lunch. She **chatted** at the table with Mrs. Crumm and her sister and took no notice of Hattie. She sat opposite Alice, silent and **restless**, but she was not at all sorry for what she had done. She could have **endured** days of **indifference** on Alice's part, without feeling the slightest **remorse**.

It was a beautiful day. After lunch, they went with Mrs. Crumm, her sister, and the hotel hostess, Mrs. Holland, and sat in Gramercy Park.

Alice pretended to be absorbed in her book. It was a detective story by her favorite author, **borrowed** from the hotel's **circulating library**. Mrs. Crumm and her sister did most of the talking. A weekend trip was of **sufficient** importance to **provide** a **topic** of conversation for several afternoons, and Mrs. Crumm was able to remember every item of food she ate on visits for days running.

The monotonous tones of the voices, the warmth of the sunlight **lulled** Alice into half sleep. The page was **blurred** to her eyes.

Earlier in the day she had planned to adopt an attitude toward Hattie. She should be cold and **aloof**, even **hostile**. It was not the first time Hattie had **committed** such an **outrage**. There was the ink spilt on her **lace** tablecloth four months ago, and her missing **morocco** volume of Tennyson. She was sure Hattie had it, somewhere. And that evening, she would calmly pack her bag, write Hattie a note, short but carefully worded, and leave the hotel. She could go to another hotel in the neighborhood, let it be known through Mrs. Crumm

---

to chat [tʃæt] plaudern **restless** ['restləs] unruhig **to endure** [ɪn'djʊə] ertragen **indifference** [ɪn'dɪfrəns] Gleichgültigkeit **remorse** [rɪ'mɔːs] Reue, Gewissensbisse **borrowed** ['bɒrəʊd] ausgeliehen **circulating library** ['sɜːkjʊleɪtɪŋ 'laɪbrərɪ] Leihbücherei **sufficient** [sə'fɪʃnt] ausreichend **to provide** [prə'vaɪd] liefern **topic** ['tɒpɪk] Thema **to lull** [lʌl] einschläfern **blurred** [blɜːd] verschwommen **aloof** [ə'luːf] reserviert **hostile** ['hɒstaɪl] feindselig **to commit** [kə'mɪt] begehen **outrage** ['aʊtreɪdʒ] Schandtat **lace** [leɪs] Spitze **morocco** [mə'rɒkəʊ] Marokkoleder

where she was, and have the satisfaction of Hattie's coming to her and apologizing. But the fact of it was, she was not at all sure that Hattie would come to her, and this **embarrassing** possibility, plus a characteristic **lack of enterprise prevented** her taking such a dangerous course... . What if she had to spend the rest of her life alone? ... It was much easier to stay where she was, to have a pleasant game of rummy in the afternoon, with ice cream and cookies, and to take out her **revenge** in little ways. It was also more ladylike, she **consoled** herself. She did not think beyond this, of the particular situations when she would say or do things calculated to hurt Hattie. The opportunities would just come of themselves.

Mrs. Holland **nudged** her. "We're going to get some ice cream now. Then we're going to play some rummy."

"I was just at the most exciting part of the book." But she rose with the others and was almost **cheerful** as they walked to the drug store.

She won at rummy, too, and she felt pleased with herself. Hattie, watching her uneasily all day, was much relieved when Alice **decreed speaking terms** again.

Nevertheless, the thought of the ruined sweater **rankled** in Alice's mind, **prodded** her with a sense of injustice. Indeed, she was ashamed of herself for being able to consider it as lightly as she did. It was letting Hattie walk over her. She wished she could **muster** a really strong **hatred**.

They were in their room reading at nine o'clock. Every **vestige** of Hattie's shyness or **pretended contrition** had **vanished**.

"Wasn't it a nice day?" she **ventured**.

---

embarrassing [ɪm'bærəsɪŋ] peinlich **lack of enterprise** [ˌlæk əv 'entəpraɪz] Mangel an Initiative **to prevent** [prɪ'vent] hindern **revenge** [rɪ'vendʒ] Rache **to console** [kən'səʊl] trösten **to nudge** [nʌdʒ] anstupsen **cheerful** ['tʃɪəfl] fröhlich **to decree speaking terms** [dɪ'kriː 'spiːkɪŋ tɜːmz] sich herablassen, mit j-m zu sprechen **to rankle** ['ræŋkl] eitern, schwären **to prod** [prɒd] anstoßen, antreiben **to muster** ['mʌstə] aufbieten **hatred** ['heɪtrɪd] Hass **vestige** ['vestɪdʒ] Spur **pretended** [prɪ'tendɪd] vorgetäuscht **contrition** [kən'trɪʃn] Reue **to vanish** ['vænɪʃ] verschwinden **to venture** ['ventʃə] etw. zu sagen wagen

"H-m-m." Alice did not raise her head.

"Well," she made the **inevitable** remark through the inevitable **yawn**, "I reckon I'll be going off to bed."

And a few minutes later they were both in bed, propped up by four pillows, reading; Hattie with the newspaper and Alice with her detective story. They were silent for a while, then Hattie adjusted her pillows and lay down.

"Good night, Alice."

"Good night."

Soon Alice pulled out the light, and there was absolute silence in the room except for the soft ticking of the clock and the **occasional** purr of an automobile. The **timepiece** on the **mantel whirred** and then began to strike ten.

Alice lay open-eyed. All day her tears had been **restrained** and now, automatically, she began to cry. She wiped her nose on the top of the sheet. But they were not childish tears.

She raised herself on one elbow. The darkish braid of hair outlined Hattie's neck and shoulder against the white bedclothes. She felt very strong, strong enough to murder Hattie with her own hands. But the idea of murder passed from her mind as swiftly as it had entered. Her revenge had to be something that would last, that would hurt, something that Hattie must endure and that she, Alice, could enjoy.

Then it came to her, and she was out of bed, walking **boldly** to the sewing table as Hattie had done twenty-four hours before ... and she was standing by the bed, bending over Hattie, peering at her **placid**, innocent face through her tears

---

inevitable [ɪn'evɪtəbl] unvermeidlich **yawn** [jɔːn] Gähnen **occasional** [ə'keɪʒnəl] gelegentlich **timepiece** ['taɪmpiːs] Uhr **mantel** *i.e.* **mantlepiece** ['mæntl(piːs)] Kaminsims **to whir** [wɜː] surren **restrained** [rɪ'streɪnd] zurückgehalten **boldly** ['bəʊldlɪ] kühn **placid** ['plæsɪd] friedlich

and her short-sighted eyes. Two quick **strokes** could cut the braid, right near the head.

But suddenly her fingers were **limp**, hardly strong enough to hold the scissors, much less **slice** through a **rope** of hair.

She steadied herself on the bed table ... Hattie, dear Hattie ... Hattie meant well. Hattie was just **mischievous**. She laid the scissors on the table and gave a great sob.

Hattie yawned and squinted her eyes open.

"I ... I was just getting a drink of water," Alice said. She moved toward the basin.

Hattie yawned and grunted.

"Would you like some?"

"I don't mind if I do," Hattie murmured.

She brought her a **tumbler** half full, and Hattie took it without a word as a child would. Alice felt her way around the bed and climbed in. She lay there looking at the ceiling with **sore tear-pink** eyes, and after a moment she heard Hattie set the glass down on the table.

---

stroke [strəʊk] Schnitt **limp** [lɪmp] schlaff **to slice** [slaɪs] schneiden **rope** [rəʊp] Strang **mischievous** ['mɪstʃɪvəs] schelmisch **tumbler** ['tʌmblə] Trinkbecher **sore** [sɔː] wund **tear-pink** ['tɪəpɪŋk] von Tränen gerötet

Born Failure

Some men are born to success as the **sparks** fly upward. Some men start making a profit on penny lemonades at the age of five, gather a little **backlog swapping** old cars at fifteen, and by fifty the thousands are **gushing** in from oil, cotton, babies' **didy** services, frozen **cheese blintzes**, or whatever else they have **applied**, however casually, their golden-touched **brains to**.

Such was not Winthrop Hazlewood. Winnie was a born failure. He looked like a failure even at the age of five, sitting with his big brother (who looked like a success at the age of ten) in a **goat-cart** photograph that still stands on the piano in Winnie's house in Bingley, Vermont. There is another picture on the piano showing Winnie at twenty-one with his college mates on **graduation day**, Winnie fifth from the left in the back row, **hangdog** and **unobtrusive**, as if he were actually ashamed of the occasion that caused him to be photographed that day.

But Winnie had an **aspiration**, even at twenty-one. He wanted to open a **general store**. It was characteristic of Winnie that he never spoke of it as a "department store" but as a "general store." Winnie wanted to live in a small town. His idea was to learn the business by **clerking** in a department store in Bennington, his hometown, and then open a store for himself. In his seventh year of clerking, his fiancée, Rose Adams, got tired of waiting for him to learn the business and **yanked** him **from** the job and from Bennington to Bingley-on-the-Dardle, where Winnie had always said he wanted to

---

failure ['feɪljə] Versager **spark** [spɑːk] Funke **backlog** ['bæklɒg] *hier:* finanzielles Polster **to swap** [swɒp] eintauschen **to gush** [gʌʃ] sprudeln **didy** *coll. für* **diaper** ['daɪdɪ] Windel **cheese blintz** ['tʃiːz blɪnts] Käsegebäck **to apply one's brain to s.th.** [ə'plaɪ, breɪn] sich gedanklich befassen mit **goat-cart** ['gəʊtkɑːt] von einer Ziege gezogener Wagen **graduation day** [ˌgrædʒʊ'eɪʃn deɪ] (amerik.) Schulabschlussfeier **hangdog** ['hæŋdɒg] trübsinnig **unobtrusive** [ˌʌnəb'truːsɪv] unaufdringlich **aspiration** [ˌæspə'reɪʃn] Ziel **general store** ['dʒenrəl stɔː] Gemischtwarenladen **to clerk** [klɑːk] als Gehilfe arbeiten **to yank s.o. from** [jæŋk] j-n wegreißen von

live. Winnie had a little money saved up, and Rose's father gave her a thousand dollars as a **dowry**, plus another thousand exclusively for the new store. It took Winnie over five years to pay the thousand dollars back to Mr. Adams with interest. By that time, Winnie's first and last child, Mary, had been born and had died in the second month of its life. The doctor said that Rose should never try to have another. Winnie was deeply disappointed, because he loved children, but he never showed his disappointment to Rose. Winnie was a man of resignation.

Winnie had wanted a store that specialized in men's clothing, especially workingmen's clothing, because Bingley was a farm community, and in such things as **ribbons**, buttons, nails, and hammers—the kind of things people needed every day, Winnie said. It didn't take Rose a minute to see that two other stores took care of Bingley's needs in these lines, but that what the town **lacked** was a good dry goods store. So Winnie took her **advice** and concentrated on dry goods, from cottons up to heavy woolens. He also sold some **haberdashery**, soaps, **stationery**, toys, overshoes, **percolators**, and floor wax. These last stocks **varied**, because Winnie was a great one for buying a **bargain** in any line of goods when a salesman offered it to him. And the **stocks** moved very slowly for the reason, as Rose always pointed out, that people never knew what he had at any certain time. If they came back to buy a second box of soap, for instance, there wouldn't be any more in stock, no soap at all, which didn't make for **steady** customers. The women of Bingley all **sewed**, but there just weren't enough of

---

dowry ['daʊrɪ] Mitgift **ribbon** ['rɪbən] Band, Borte **to lack** [læk] nicht haben **advice** [əd'vaɪs] Rat **haberdashery** [ˌhæbə'dæʃərɪ] Kurzwaren **stationery** ['steɪʃənrɪ] Papierwaren **percolator** ['pɜːkəleɪtə] Kaffeemaschine **to vary** ['veərɪ] abwechseln **bargain** ['bɑːgən] Schnäppchen **stocks** *Pl.* [stɒks] Vorräte **steady** ['stedɪ] gleichmäßig, regelmäßig **to sew** [səʊ] nähen

them to make Winnie rich. Winnie was fifty-two, and a tired, **skinny** old man, before he paid off his two-story house on Independence Street.

And even that was **at the expense of** not getting his store painted, or **reroofed**, or the cellar waterproofed, or anything else that a respectable **emporium** needs. Like Winnie, the old middle-sized **cracker box** of a store on the river side of Main Street looked a lot older than it was. The reddish paint had **weathered** to a **mottled** brown, and nearly all the **gilt** letters on the sign in front that said HAZLEWOOD'S GENERAL **MERCHANDISE** had chipped off so that you couldn't read them unless you knew what they were supposed to say. Yet the store had become a **fixture** in the town, and most Bingley women wouldn't buy their materials anywhere else, even in Bennington. As low as Winnie's cash reserves got sometimes, they never quite went down to zero, and he and Rose managed to eat, though not much by the looks of Winnie. He was about the size of a skinny fourteen-year-old boy, not very tall and inclined to **stoop**. He had a clean-shaven, completely forgettable face—a nose that was just a nose, a mouth as gentle as a sheep's, and steady but tired gray eyes that looked out from under very ordinary brown eyebrows. His father had grown **bald** early, but Winnie's **straight** brown-and-gray hair grew **tenaciously**, as thick as it had ever been, parted on the left and hanging over his forehead a little, as it had since he was a small boy. In a bigger town, few people would ever have noticed Winnie, but in Bingley everybody knew him and spoke to him on the street, as if in a town of Bingley's smallness Winnie had become dis-

---

skinny ['skɪnɪ] dünn **at the expense of** [ɪk'spens] auf Kosten von **to reroof** [rɪ'ru:f] neu eindecken (Hausdach) **emporium** [em'pɔ:rɪəm] Kaufhaus **cracker box** ['krækə bɒks] *etwa:* Bruchbude **to weather** ['weðə] verwittern **mottled** ['mɒtld] gefleckt **gilt** [gɪlt] golden **merchandise** ['mɜ:tʃəndaɪz] Ware **fixture** ['fɪkstʃə] fester Bestandteil **to stoop** [stu:p] nach vorne geneigt gehen **bald** [bɔ:ld] kahl **straight** [streɪt] gerade **tenaciously** [tə'neɪʃəslɪ] beharrlich

tinctive just for ordinariness. His bookkeeping kept him at the store until nine o'clock and after in the evenings, about the time when Bingley's young men were walking their girls home from the seven o'clock movie at the Orpheus. All of them said hello to Winnie if they passed him, or if the light was still on in the back room of the store they would say, "I guess Winnie's still at it, poor old guy." And if they didn't see him, and saw no light, they would remark that Winnie must be home early **for a change**. In short, Winnie was not really a forgotten man in Bingley, not a **cog** in a machine the way a lot of big-city **dwellers** are. But Winnie was very much aware that he hadn't gotten half as far as most men in Bingley, though he worked twice as hard as most.

Besides **having a streak of middling to bad luck** for years and years, Winnie had a few **misfortunes** that were **plain unusual**. Like the time his older brother turned up in Bingley, fifty years old and **flat broke**. The last Winnie had heard of Richard, he had made a quarter of a million dollars on the **stock market** playing Mexican mines. Richard had written him a triumphant letter about that, and had said he was off to Mexico to buy himself a village to retire in. But the Richard that turned up in Bingley was a shadow of his old self. He had put all his money into a silver mine that never produced, had sold **at a loss**, and then lost that money at a **gambling casino** in Mexico City. Richard asked Winnie for a job in his store. Winnie said he could put him up at the house all right, but he couldn't possibly take him on at the store. There wasn't enough work, and there wasn't enough money coming in to pay a **salary** with. But Richard **pled** with him.

---

for a change [tʃeɪndʒ] ausnahmsweise **cog** [kɒg] Rädchen (im Getriebe) **dweller** ['dwelə] Bewohner **to have a streak of middling to bad luck** [striːk, 'mɪdlɪŋ, lʌk] immer wieder ziemlich viel Pech haben **misfortune** [ˌmɪs'fɔːtʃən] Missgeschick **plain unusual** [pleɪn ʌn'juːʒʊəl] wirklich ungewöhnlich **flat broke** [flæt brəʊk] vollkommen pleite **stock market** ['stɒk ˌmɑːkɪt] Börse **at a loss** [lɒs] mit Verlust **gambling casino** ['gæmblɪŋ kəˌsiːnəʊ] Spielbank **salary** ['sælərɪ] Lohn **pled** *Pret.* **to plead** [pled, pliːd] inständig bitten

"Can you do bookkeeping?" Winnie asked.

"Anything! Sure I can do bookkeeping, Winnie. Figures were always my specialty, don't you remember?" Richard made **wavy** gestures with his hands, and a ghost of his **jaunty** smile came back.

"I sure do need a bookkeeper," Winnie said. "But I couldn't pay you more than … say, twenty-five dollars a week."

Richard said that was fine. "I'll help you out with the clerking, too," Richard said.

Rose was furious with Winnie. "Richard, who's never given you a cent!" Rose said.

"Well, I never asked him for any," Winnie replied.

"I bet he can't add six and four! He never could do anything but sport around and **blow his own horn**!" And Rose would have said a lot more, if she hadn't been glad, in a way, that Winnie was taking on a bookkeeper, even a bad one. It hurt Rose that everybody in Bingley talked about Winnie's not having a single clerk in the store, and coming home late at night summer and winter because he had to stay late totaling up his own **accounts**. Rose had had high aspirations when they first came to Bingley. Gradually she had **turned loose of** most of them, but she still **longed for** a refrigerator and a new sewing machine that worked by electricity. Now, what with paying Richard twenty-five dollars in cash every week, it was hopeless to dream of a refrigerator and a sewing machine **anyways** soon.

Richard **had no knack** at all for bookkeeping, or even arithmetic. He would sit bent over his desk in the back corner of the store all day, apparently working with his pen, but ac-

---

wavy ['weɪvɪ] wellenförmig **jaunty** ['dʒɔːntɪ] fröhlich **to blow one's own horn** [bləʊ, hɔːn] sich selbst loben **account** [ə'kaʊnt] Buchführung **to turn loose of s.th.** [tɜːn 'luːs] etw. aufgeben **to long for** [lɒŋ] sich sehnen nach **anyways** ['enɪweɪz] jedenfalls **to have a knack for s.th.** [næk] e-e Begabung haben für

tually just **doodling** in the **margins**, and **scheming up** ways to make another pot of easy money and move on to a **gayer** place than Bingley. Far from helping Winnie with the clerking, on the rare occasions when there was more than one person in the store, Richard would choose these times to disappear entirely, sometimes into the bathroom, sometimes out the back door for a walk. He was trying to build up some social contacts in Bingley, and he did not want everybody in town to know that he was working for his brother. If Richard ever approached a **counter**, it was to pick out a new tie for himself, or to get himself a clean pair of socks.

So it was not long before Winnie was doing his own bookkeeping again, and **trudging** home through knee-deep snow at ten o'clock at night, so bent over with **fatigue** that he looked smaller and more **insignificant** than ever. But Winnie never told Rose that Richard was not doing well, and he continued to pay Richard twenty-five dollars a week for practically nothing. And Rose asked only ten dollars a week for his **room and board**, though Richard ate more than she and Winnie put together. Richard **gained weight** and the color came back to his face.

"I don't expect he'll be with us much longer," Winnie said.

"Did he say when he was leaving?" Rose asked hopefully.

"**Nope**, but I can tell."

"You'd just better **search** him the day he takes off," Rose warned Winnie.

But that would not have done any good, because Richard departed one day—and Winnie and Rose **saw** him **off** at the

---

to doodle ['du:dl] kritzeln **margin** ['mɑ:dʒɪn] (Seiten-)Rand **to scheme up s.th.** [ski:m] sich etw. ausdenken **gay** [geɪ] lustig, fröhlich **counter** ['kaʊntə] Ladentisch **to trudge** [trʌdʒ] stapfen **fatigue** [fə'ti:g] Müdigkeit **insignificant** [ˌɪnsɪg'nɪfɪkənt] unbedeutend **room and board** [ˌru:m ən 'bɔ:d] Kost und Logis **to gain weight** [geɪn 'weɪt] zunehmen **nope** *i.e.* **no** [nəʊp] **to search s.o.** [sɜ:tʃ] j-n durchsuchen **to see s.o. off** [si: ... 'ɒf] j-n verabschieden

station and gave him a box lunch of fried chicken and angel food cake—in possession of **valuables** that could not have been **detected** on him: seven hundred fifty dollars **transferred** from Winnie's store accounts to a bank in New York City. Winnie did not discover this loss for nearly a month. And he kept it a secret from Rose.

That was near Christmas, and every year Winnie had been in Bingley he had managed to set aside a hundred dollars or so for a Christmas party and presents for the children at the county **orphanage** a few miles out of town. These parties always cleaned out his stock of toys at the store, too. That year, even with the loss of Richard's seven hundred fifty dollars to be covered, Winnie managed to **scrape up** a hundred in cash to buy **candy** and **cookies** and to hire the **sleigh** and horses in which he gave all the orphans rides in groups of six and eight. Rose did not **begrudge** the money Winnie spent on the children's Christmas. She loved to see Winnie's skinny, tired face light up when he sat with the **reins** in his hands surrounded by children, with the breeze flattening the **fur** of his **raccoon** cap as he **clucked** up the horses to a good lively trot. Rose knew how much he missed having children of his own.

There was a heavy fall of snow the winter that Richard came and went, and an early **thaw** that **caught** everybody **unawares**, and Winnie more than anybody. About three thousand dollars' worth of woolens, cottons, denim shirts, nails, and whatever else happened to be stored around the walls of the cellar got ruined by **mildew** and **rust**. It wasn't only the thaw, of course. Winnie's cellar had always been damp. Winnie had been

---

valuable ['væljʊəbl] Wertgegenstand **to detect** [dɪ'tekt] entdecken **to transfer** [træns'fɜː] überweisen **orphanage** ['ɔːfənɪdʒ] Waisenhaus **to scrape up** [skreɪp] zusammenkratzen **candy** ['kændɪ] Süßigkeiten **cooky** ['kʊkɪ] Keks **sleigh** [sleɪ] Schlitten **to begrudge s.o. s.th.** [bɪ'grʌdʒ] j-m etw. missgönnen **rein** [reɪn] Zügel **fur** [fɜː] Fell **raccoon** [rə'kuːn] Waschbär **to cluck** [klʌk] (mit der Zunge) schnalzen **thaw** [θɔː] Tauwetter **to catch s.o. unawares** [ˌkætʃ … ˌʌnə'weəz] j-n überraschen **mildew** ['mɪldjuː] Schimmel **rust** [rʌst] Rost

going to have it recemented, but he had never seen his way clear to spending that amount of money. Now it was too late. Winnie expected Rose to **fly off the handle** about the cellar, because she had been after him to have it repaired for years. But she didn't. She just put her arm around him and patted his shoulder, without saying a word. Rose's patience with him that day **affected** Winnie so much that tears came to his eyes.

"Don't you worry, Rose. I'll make up for it this year," Winnie promised.

A few months later, when a salesman from New Haven told him about a cotton shipment from India that he could have for less than a third of its actual value, Winnie thought that his opportunity to **recoup** his losses had come. The salesmen had a **sample** of the material.

"Only one thousand dollars," the salesman said. "The only trouble is that the **cargo** isn't **insured**. The company in India has just gone bankrupt and they haven't a cent."

Winnie thought about this. He decided to be on the safe side. "I'll insure it from here," he said. "How soon will they be able to send it?"

"It's already on the way. **It's due** in another three weeks, via Suez and Gibraltar. You'd be buying moving cargo."

Winnie could see no **advantage** in buying moving cargo, but the salesman seemed to think he should. The only advantage was the low price, and even Winnie was enough of a businessman to know why it was low.

"**Are** you **game** to take a gamble? Cash on the line now?"

"Yes," Winnie said. He paid the salesman seventy-five in cash, and the rest in a check on his bank in Bingley, which **granted** him a **loan**.

---

to fly off the handle *coll.* ['hændl] an die Decke gehen **to affect** [ə'fekt] (be-)rühren **to recoup** [rɪ'kuːp] wieder gutmachen, aufholen **sample** ['sɑːmpl] Probe **cargo** ['kɑːgəʊ] Ladung **insured** [ɪn'ʃʊəd] versichert **to be due** [djuː] zu erwarten sein **advantage** [əd'vɑːntɪdʒ] Vorteil **to be game to do s.th.** [geɪm] bereit sein etw. zu tun **to grant** [grɑːnt] gewähren **loan** [ləʊn] Kredit

Three weeks to the day after the transaction, Winnie received a letter from the salesman saying that the **freighter** *Bena-Li* out of Calcutta, bound for Gibraltar, had caught fire in the Mediterranean and sunk. Rose made him take steps to investigate the fire. The salesman never replied to Winnie's letter, but the Port Authority of New York confirmed the fact that a ship of that name had sunk in the Mediterranean on the date the salesman said. Its cargo, said the letter, was raw cotton, bamboo, and some tea. No cloth was mentioned.

"It's my opinion there never was any cloth anywhere," Rose said. "Why would the salesman have had one little piece of it in Vermont to show you?"

Winnie knew she was probably right. He stood in the middle of the living room, too ashamed of himself to say anything.

"Do you know what I think you should do? Take a good long **vacation**," Rose said. "Go up to Maine and do some fishing. Remember how you used to talk about going to Maine for some fishing?"

Winnie barely remembered. He had not dreamt of taking a vacation in years. He could not remember the last vacation he'd had. "I don't **deserve** it, Rose."

"But it'd do you so much good. Just close up the store and go, Winnie. This very month!"

Winnie said he might in the latter part of July. Then in August, and then in September. And then he never did. He was worried about the loan he had to pay back to the bank. Winnie went on working from seven in the morning till ten at night, sorting stocks, making change, renewing orders in cautious quantities, and totaling up at the end of the day his intakes of $6.25, $11.19, and sometimes only $3.10.

---

freighter ['freɪtə] Frachter **vacation** [və'keɪʃn] Urlaub **to deserve s.th.** [dɪ'zɜːv] etw. verdienen

One evening he picked up the **antimacassar** that lay on the back of his armchair, and it fell apart in his fingers. Rather, it **dissolved** in his fingers, like so much smoke. He dropped the weightless fragments into the **wastebasket**. They were so fine, he doubted that Rose would even notice them when she emptied the basket.

Five more years passed, and in spite of many little ups and downs, Winnie's bank account stayed around a hundred and seventy-five dollars, just about what it had been after Richard **absconded** with the seven hundred fifty. The only thing that changed was Rose's hair, which got grayer and grayer, and the sensations in Winnie's legs as he trudged home in the winter evenings, lifting his feet high to get through the snow. Winnie felt tireder every winter.

Then one day in April, when Winnie was sixty-one, a letter came from a **lawyers'** firm in New York. It said that Oliver Hazlewood, an old uncle of Winnie's, had died and left him a hundred thousand dollars in his **will**. It would take a year to **probate** the will, but after taxes and legal **fees**, Winthrop Hazlewood would receive eighty thousand.

Winnie and Rose took this news very calmly, because neither of them could quite realize it was true. They didn't even talk about the money for days. Finally Rose broke the silence by speaking of old Oliver Hazlewood, whom she had met only once, at her wedding. Rose said it was very nice of him to have remembered Winnie so well, since as far as she knew Winnie had never been close to him, had he? Winnie said he hadn't been at all close to him, and that he was very **touched** at Uncle Oliver's giving him all that.

A little later, they began to talk of what they would do when the money came. They would go to Florida for a vaca-

---

antimacassar [ˌæntɪməˈkæsə] Sesselschoner **to dissolve** [dɪˈzɒlv] sich auflösen **wastebasket** [ˈweɪstbɑːskɪt] Papierkorb **to abscond** [əbˈskɒnd] abhauen **lawyer** [ˈlɔːjə] Rechtsanwalt **will** [wɪl] Testament **to probate** [ˈprəʊbeɪt] gerichtlich bestätigen **fees** *Pl.* [fiːz] Kosten **touched** [tʌtʃt] gerührt

tion. Or perhaps to California. They might even buy a *house* in Florida or California.

"That'd mean selling the store," Winnie said.

Both of them sat kind of **stunned** for a minute, trying to imagine a life without the store.

"We're getting on, Rose. We'd best enjoy to the full what's left of our lives," Winnie said **courageously**.

Rose tried to imagine enjoying the rest of her life to the full. Lemonade in a **hammock** somewhere. All the new dresses she wanted. Bridge parties with tea and candy like she read about. But Rose didn't know how to play bridge. Sea voyages... . There were so many things she could do, Rose got dizzy as soon as she started to think about them.

They decided that when the money came next May, they would sell the store and the house, take a slow trip by train along the border of Canada, which they had always wanted to see, and then go to California. They didn't know exactly where, but they had heard of beautiful little towns along the coast south of Los Angeles. By the time next summer rolled around, they would have a better idea as to which town would most likely **suit** them.

Christmas found Winnie as **pinched** as ever, but he rented the sleigh, loaded it with presents for the orphans, and drove out to the orphanage for a Christmas Eve afternoon like all the thirty-odd others he had spent in Bingley. But this time there was a surprise for Winnie.

Above the gates of the orphanage **fluttered** a red **streamer** with gold letters, saying, MERRY CHRISTMAS, WINNIE!

All the children were waiting for him on the orphanage steps, and Sister Josephine, the superintendent, was there, too. Sister Josephine came forward as soon as Winnie drew rein and handed him a little box.

---

stunned [stʌnd] fassungslos **courageously** [kə'reɪdʒəslɪ] mutig **hammock** ['hæmək] Hängematte **to suit s.o.** [suːt] j-m passen, angenehm sein **pinched** [pɪntʃt] knapp bei Kasse **to flutter** ['flʌtə] flattern **streamer** ['striːmə] Spruchband

"The children made up a collection to buy you this for Christmas, Winnie," Sister Josephine said. "They asked me to give it to you, but it's their present, every bit of it."

Winnie opened the box. Inside was a gold watch, engraved with flowery **scrolls** on the cover that flipped open to show the watch face. On the back, it was engraved with his **intertwined initials**.

"Merry Christmas, Winnie!" the children yelled.

Winnie was **blushing.** All he could think of was that the children had **donated** thousands of precious pennies to buy the expensive watch, and that he was soon going to be so rich, he could easily buy himself a watch like this and not even feel it. He decided he must talk to Sister Josephine in private, tell her about the money he was going to get, and ask her to sell the watch and return the money to the children. But that could wait a few days, until after Christmas, of course.

Winnie showed the watch to Rose. Rose told him he ought to keep it, no matter what. It was the sentiment **attached** to it, not so much the money, she said.

"Besides, you wouldn't want everybody in town to know we're going to get all that money—yet—would you?"

Winnie certainly didn't. The eighty thousand dollars put him into an **agony** of **shyness** every time he thought about it. They would have to tell everybody eventually, of course, but Winnie wanted it to be at the last moment, and as quietly as possible.

"Sister Josephine can keep a secret, though," Winnie said. "I ought to give the watch back soon, so they can get the same price they paid for it."

Rose saw there was no **arguing with** him, either about keeping the watch or talking to Sister Josephine right away.

---

scroll [skrəʊl] Schnörkelverzierung **intertwined initials** [ˌɪntə'twaɪnd ɪ'nɪʃlz] ineinander verschlungene Initialen **to blush** [blʌʃ] erröten **to donate** [dəʊ'neɪt] spenden **to attach s.th. to s.th.** [ə'tætʃ] etw. verbinden mit **agony** ['ægənɪ] Qual **shyness** ['ʃaɪnəs] Scheu, peinliche Berührtheit **to argue with s.o.** ['ɑːgjuː] sich mit j-m auseinandersetzen

Winnie went to Sister Josephine on the second of January, and asked her to take the watch back. Sister Josephine wanted him to keep the watch and give its value back in money, when he got his money. But Winnie couldn't bring himself to wait till May.

"It's going to make the children very disappointed," she told him.

"I hope not for long," Winnie said. Then he **crept** out of her office, bent and small and more **humble** in his heart than any child who had ever crept out of Sister Josephine's office after being **scolded**.

May came around finally, and Winnie got a letter from Mr. Hughes of the law firm, asking him to come to New York to sign some papers and to receive the money.

"Well, I suppose it's time we told Ed we want to put the house and the store up for sale," Winnie said. Ed Stevens was the **real estate agent** in Bingley.

"I suppose it is," Rose said.

Winnie spoke to Ed that afternoon, and told him the reason: he was going to get eighty thousand dollars, and he and Rose were going to live in California. Within an hour, the news was all over town. That afternoon, Winnie's store was **jammed** with people coming in to congratulate him and shake his hand. Winnie thought from their smiles that they meant it, too. He had been worried that some people might be **envious**.

The next day, Winnie went to New York. It was only the second time in his life he had been to the big town. The first time he had been so small he couldn't remember much, so it was a brand-new experience to him, and just riding by taxi—Winnie

---

crept *Pret.* **to creep** [krept, kriːp] schleichen **humble** [ˈhʌmbl] demütig **to scold** [skəʊld] tadeln, schelten **real estate agent** [ˈrɪəl‿ɪˌsteɪt ˌeɪdʒənt] Immobilienmakler **jammed** [dʒæmd] vollgestopft **envious** [ˈenvɪəs] neidisch

would have walked but he was afraid of getting lost and being late for the **appointment** with Mr. Hughes—from Grand Central Station to East Fifty-second Street made Winnie feel like a piece of **pine** he had watched once being shot through a **sawmill** in Bennington, **barked**, dressed, and cut up for kitchen **matches** in less time than it takes to tell. Winnie felt about as insignificant as a kitchen match when he walked into Mr. Hughes's **plush-carpeted** office. But Mr. Hughes was awfully friendly and nice to him, and explained what all the papers were before he signed them, as if Winnie were quite familiar with such matters.

"What bank would you like the eighty thousand **deposited** in, Mr. Hazlewood?" the lawyer asked. "Or do you want the whole thing **in trust**?"

Winnie **gulped**, thinking of eighty thousand dollars landing in the Bingley Bank. "My wife and I are going right off to Canada," Winnie said. "Then we're going to California to stay, so we'll be giving up our present bank. I don't suppose you could give me the money in cash, could you?"

Mr. Hughes looked surprised for a minute, then he smiled and said, "Why, yes, we could by this afternoon. But are you sure you want to risk carrying all that with you to Vermont, just in your pocket?"

Winnie had with him an old **briefcase** in which he had intended to carry the money away. "I never lost a **dime** in my life just by leaving it somewheres. Or even by getting robbed," Winnie added with a smile.

So Winnie arranged to come back to Mr. Hughes's office at four, which would still give him time to catch the **sleeper** at five-thirty for Vermont. Winnie passed the time by walking

---

appointment [ə'pɔɪntmənt] Verabredung **pine** [paɪn] Fichte(nholz) **sawmill** ['sɔːmɪl] Sägewerk **barked** [bɑːkt] geschält, abgerindet **match** [mætʃ] Streichholz **plush-carpeted** ['plʌʃˌkɑːpɪtɪd] mit dicken Teppichen ausgelegt **to deposit** [dɪ'pɒzɪt] (Geld) einzahlen **in trust** [trʌst] zur (treuhänderischen) Verwahrung **to gulp** [gʌlp] schlucken **briefcase** ['briːfkeɪs] Aktentasche **dime** [daɪm] Zehncentstück **sleeper** ['sliːpə] Schlafwagen

slowly up Fifth Avenue, which he knew was the most famous street, looking wonderingly at the big buses, the taxis that raced by painted every color in the rainbow, and at the shop windows full of expensive articles. Winnie was attracted by a pair of binoculars priced at eighty-five dollars. He looked at them with a vague longing, and from the great distance of the **unattainable**, just as he had looked all his life at every costly object that he would have liked to possess. Then suddenly he realized that he could buy them by this afternoon at four. Why, eighty-five dollars was only about one *thousandth* of the money he would have! The idea made Winnie feel light in the head, and he walked on up the avenue, trying to **get his bearings** by thinking of something else. He sat for a while in Central Park. The trees looked pretty **puny**, but he felt better surrounded by the green things than by all the concrete buildings.

At a little after four, Mr. Hughes handed Winnie eight packets of banknotes, each one containing ten one-thousand dollar bills. The bills didn't even look like money with those little 1000 figures in the corners, but Winnie's hands were **trembling** as he put the packets into the briefcase. Mr. Hughes shook his hand warmly, and wished him a glorious time in Canada and California. Winnie thanked him very kindly, both for himself and for Rose.

Winnie tried not to think about the money on the train. He just put the briefcase in the net over his head in the upper **berth**, and fell asleep about as quickly as he usually did.

It was only the next morning, on the ferry across the Dardle to Bingley, that Winnie began to think about the money in the briefcase. He thought about how hard he had worked all his life, and how little he had ever made. Not even enough to buy

---

unattainable [ˌʌnəˈteɪnəbl] unerreichbar **to get one's bearings** [ˈbeərɪŋz] sich zurechtfinden **puny** [ˈpjuːnɪ] mickerig **to tremble** [ˈtrembl] zittern **berth** [bɜːθ] Schlafwagenbett, Koje

Rose a refrigerator yet. He thought about all the mistakes he had made, and the bad luck that had followed him like a hound dog on a sure **trail**, ever since he had come to Bingley—his brother's going off with all that money, and the mildew in the cellar, and all the times he couldn't even count when he had bought goods that wouldn't sell, when he had given the wrong people credit, and all the times he had *not* bought certain goods that would have sold and made some money if he had bought them. It was just as if he had *looked* for failure all his life, he thought, and as if *finding* failure was the only thing he had ever done successfully. And now he'd been handed a fortune on a **silver platter**, eighty thousand dollars for doing absolutely nothing. He didn't deserve it. It didn't seem fated, this piece of luck that was going to change his life completely. Winnie reached for a handkerchief in his hip pocket. He was thinking about leaving Bingley, and there were tears in his eyes. Just as he brought the handkerchief up, his hand hit the briefcase, which was lying on the **rail** of the ferry.

Winnie **grabbed for** it, but he was too late. The briefcase dropped down and down and fell with a quiet plop into the water. Winnie leaned over the rail. It was gone without a trace.

"Hey!" Winnie yelled up at the bridge. "Say, stop the boat! I just lost eighty thousand dollars!"

"Lost what?" asked one of the passengers on the deck, a man Winnie didn't know.

Winnie headed for the steps that went up to the bridge. Then he stopped, shaking from head to foot. It was silly to think of stopping the boat. The way the river was rushing by—high water, too, **swirly** and full of mud from the spring rains—he'd never get that briefcase back in a thousand years, not even if he hired a crew of divers to go down and look for it!

---

trail [treɪl] Spur, Fährte **silver platter** [ˌsɪlvə ˈplætə] Silbertablett
rail [reɪl] Reling **to grab for** [græb] greifen nach **swirly** [ˈswɜːlɪ] aufgewühlt

"*What* did you say you lost?" asked the man beside him.

"Nothing," Winnie said.

The boat was drawing near the Bingley slip. There seemed to be a lot of people down at the dock. Winnie had hoped he could get home unseen by anybody, because he knew the first person who saw him coming back from New York was going to rush up and congratulate him on having the money. Now he knew he couldn't. Just as he stepped on the **gangplank**, a roar went up from the crowd.

"Welcome home, Winnie!"

"How's the millionaire?"

"Where's your Rolls-Royce, Winnie?"

The firemen's band by the boathouse started playing "There'll Be a Hot Time in the Old Town Tonight," loud enough to **drown out** all the yelling and cheering, and Winnie saw Rose, all dressed up in her Sunday best, with flowers pinned on her shoulder. Now everybody was yelling, *"Speech! Speech!"* Winnie walked down the gangplank toward Rose. He felt like a whipped dog, and he supposed he looked like one, but nobody seemed to gather anything from that fact.

Cal Whiting, president of the Bingley Bank, held up his hand for silence.

Winnie **braced** himself. Now was as good a time as any, Winnie told himself. They'd all know in a few hours, anyway. "Ladies and gentlemen—my old friends of Bingley," Winnie began, and loud applause followed those words. "I am deeply ashamed to tell you all that I just dropped the money over the rail of that boat there. By accident."

There was a groaning "Oh-h."

And several incredulous "Huh?"s.

"Oh, Winnie!" Rose's face had twisted up. She put out her hand as if she were going to collapse, and Winnie caught her in his arm.

---

gangplank ['gæŋplæŋk] Landungsbrücke **to drown out** [draʊn 'aʊt] ertränken, *hier:* übertönen **to brace oneself** [breɪs] sich zusammenreißen

"What you mean, Winnie?" a voice asked.

"I mean, I don't have the money anymore. I lost it all. In cash. It fell in the river. So I guess I'm just the same old failure you folks know, anyway—and I don't guess Rose and I'll be leaving Bingley."

It took the big crowd about a full minute to realize what Winnie had told them. Winnie had never felt so low, so worse than **worthless**, so unworthy of living. There they stood, he and Rose, **clinging to each other**, **defeated** again, and before the whole town for every eye to see.

Suddenly Cal Whiting said in a loud voice, "Well, folks, I think it's a cause for celebration that Winnie *isn't* leaving Bingley. What's gone is gone, so let's go on up to my house and have the party like we planned!"

Everybody agreed to that. Winnie was **whisked** like a **straw** up on the shoulders of the two or three men nearest him, and carried up Main Street and then over on Walnut toward Cal Whiting's house. Winnie lost sight of Rose, and in all the **jostling** and singing he couldn't call out for her. On the big Whiting lawn stood four or five long tables loaded with punch bowls, sandwiches, cakes, cookies, doughnuts, and candy, enough to feed the whole town, Winnie thought. All the kids from the orphanage were there, too, and Sister Josephine, smiling at him in a way that made Winnie sure she hadn't heard the bad news yet. Sister Josephine came right up to him as soon as the men put him down from their shoulders.

"Winnie—"

"Sister Josephine, I lost the money. I just told everybody about it," Winnie said in a small voice.

"I heard about it already from a little boy." Sister Josephine took his hand and pressed something into it. "I hope you'll

---

worthless [ˈwɜːθləs] unnütz **to cling to each other** [klɪŋ] sich aneinander klammern **defeated** [dɪˈfiːtɪd] (nieder)geschlagen, erfolglos **to whisk** [wɪsk] schnell mitreißen **straw** [strɔː] Strohhalm **jostling** [ˈdʒɒslɪŋ] Gedränge

keep the watch now, Winnie. I never gave it back. It's been waiting for you."

Winnie closed his hand around the watch. "Thank you, Sister Josephine."

Then they began to **ply** Winnie **with** strawberry punch and chicken sandwiches and devil's food cake, until Winnie had to retreat to a corner of the lawn for self-preservation. Rose came after him. She didn't say anything to him, just stood beside him. She was smiling, though not in the same way she had on the dock before she found out about the money.

"Are you very disappointed, Rose?" he asked her.

"I don't think I'm disappointed at all. I think today is the happiest day of my life, Winnie."

Winnie looked at her patient face. He had the feeling he'd suddenly been **reprieved** from death. But he felt he didn't deserve that, either. "You know, Rose, on the ferry this morning, just before I lost the money, I sort of *saw* myself—I mean, saw that I've been looking for failure in one way and another all my—Rose, listen for a minute."

"Come on and join the party, Winnie. We can talk later." Rose pulled at his hand.

"But I have to finish this. I want to say—"

She turned loose of his hand, and he watched her go over to one of the tables, graceful and happy-looking, almost like the day he married her. Winnie stayed where he was in the corner of the lawn. He felt strange and wonderful suddenly, as if he were twenty or thirty years younger himself.

He was having another **revelation**: he saw all his life leading up to this moment, all the years of doubt, of hopelessness, of hard, **unrewarded effort**, leading up to this moment when all the people who he hadn't known were really his friends were showing him that he had everything that he could possi-

---

to ply s.o. with s.th. [plaɪ] j-n versorgen mit **to reprieve** [rɪˈpriːv] retten, begnadigen **revelation** [ˌrevəˈleɪʃn] Enthüllung, Erkenntnis **unrewarded** [ˌʌnrɪˈwɔːdɪd] nicht belohnt **effort** [ˈefət] Mühe, Anstrengung

bly want in **abundance**. And that warmth around his heart now, the certainty that Rose loved him and that everybody in town loved him, what else had he been **seeking** all his life? What more could anybody want? Winnie wasn't worried about anything anymore. Winnie felt—he was almost ashamed even to think it about himself—successful.

---

abundance [ə'bʌndəns] Überfluss **to seek** [siːk] suchen, streben nach